T.

ROBERT N. McCAULEY

INTERNATIONAL FINANCE SECTION

DEPARTMENT OF ECONOMICS
PRINCETON UNIVERSITY
PRINCETON, NEW JERSEY

INTERNATIONAL FINANCE SECTION
EDITORIAL STAFF

Peter B. Kenen, *Director*

Margaret B. Riccardi, *Editor*

Lillian Spais, *Editorial Aide*

Lalitha H. Chandra, *Subscriptions and Orders*

Library of Congress Cataloging-in-Publication Data

McCauley, Robert N.
   The euro and the dollar / Robert N. McCauley.
   p. cm. — (Essays in international finance ; no. 205)
   Includes bibliographical references.
   ISBN 0-88165-112-5
   1. Portfolio management—European Union countries. 2. Money—European Union
countries. 3. Euro-dollar market. 4. International finance. 5. Banks and banking,
International. I. Title. II. Series.
HG4529.5.M4 1997
332.4′56094073—dc21
                                                 97-40211
                                                   CIP

Printed in the United States of America by Princeton University Printing Services at Princeton, New Jersey

International Standard Serial Number: 0071-142X
International Standard Book Number: 0-88165-112-5
Library of Congress Catalog Card Number: 97-40211

CONTENTS

FIGURES

BOX

TABLES

THE EURO AND THE DOLLAR

1 Introduction

Monetary union in Europe holds the promise of profound change for international finance. A single currency, the euro, is to circulate where powerful markets once alternated between reinforcing and opposing—and sometimes overwhelming—repeated national efforts to achieve monetary convergence. The economies sharing the euro may face the world as the largest single-currency area and the largest single trading bloc.

As this long-standing deadline has approached, it has gained credibility. Less than two years ago, the consensus drew a narrow circle around Germany's neighbors; now, the circle has widened. The quotidian poll in the bond market also shows that investors expect the euro to come—that is, bond buyers have increasingly signaled their belief that some European currencies will enjoy stability against the deutsche mark (Table 1 and Figure 1).[1]

This essay makes the assumption that the euro is coming and seeks to understand the implications of its arrival for the U.S. dollar. In particular, it investigates the motives for, and implications of, shifts of funds by international portfolio managers in response to the euro's introduction. It suggests that private portfolio shifts are likely to prove of greater importance than the much-discussed changes in the composition of central banks' foreign-exchange reserves and maintains that liability managers will play a generally overlooked role in determining the long-run relation between the dollar and the euro.

This work has benefited from discussions at the Bank for International Settlements but should be viewed as the work of the author. The author would like to thank, in particular, Svein Andresen, Steve Arthur, Florence Béranger, Henri Bernard, Joseph Bisignano, Andrew Crockett, Paul De Grauwe, Gabriele Galati, Giorgio Glinni, Serge Jeanneau, Jean-Marie Kertudo, Charles Kindleberger, Frederick Marki, Will Melick, Denis Pêtre, Georges Pineau, Fabrizio Saccomanni, Jeffrey Shafer, Frank Smets, Kostas Tsatsaronis, and William White.

[1] Figure 1 represents an implementation of the Svensson (1991) test for the credibility of exchange-rate bands. It uses private interest rates because, unlike government rates, they have similar default and country-risk characteristics; see De Grauwe (1996a) and BIS (1996b, 1997b). Lascelles (1996, p. 8) reminds us that market expectations can prove wrong.

TABLE 1

EXPECTED PARTICIPATION IN MONETARY UNION AT THE OUTSET AND SOVEREIGN CREDIT RATINGS
(in percentages)

	Poll Taken in				Foreign-Currency Rating		
Country	January 1996	August 1996	January 1997	August 1997	Moody's	S&P	IBCA
Germany	100	100	100	100	Aaa	AAA	AAA
France	97	100	100	100	Aaa	AAA	AAA
Netherlands	76	100	100	100	Aaa	AAA	AAA
Belgium	79	95	100	100	Aa1	AA+	AA+
Austria	79	93	97	96	Aaa	AAA	AAA
Ireland	60	82	88	96	Aa1	AA	AA+
Finland	36	48	76	91	Aa1	AA	AAA
Spain	7	7	31	90	Aa2	AA	AA
Portugal	0	4	32	84	Aa3	AA−	AA−
Italy	2	3	19	67	Aa3	AA	AA−
Denmark	50	43	25	16	Aa1	AA+	AA+
Sweden	7	13	13	4	Aa3	AA+	AA−
United Kingdom	22	8	4	1	Aaa	AAA	AAA
Greece	0	0	0	1	Baa1	BBB−	BBB−

SOURCES: Consensus Economics, *Consensus Forecasts*, August 1996 and 1997, p. 26; Moody's, Standard & Poor, and IBCA.

NOTE: The polls of over 200 financial and economic forecasters indicate the percentage of respondents predicting that countries will join monetary union at the outset. Respondents' assumptions regarding the likely starting date differ. Luxembourg, rated Aaa and AAA, respectively, was not included in the poll.

The burden of the essay is that the effects on the dollar of portfolio shifts in response to the arrival of the euro are easy to overstate and are often overstated. Common arguments that ascribe the dollar's strength against the mark through the summer of 1997 to the prospective introduction of the euro are one-sided. Although it may be that the prospect of the euro has led to portfolio shifts that have strengthened the dollar, it is certainly true that a cyclically strong dollar has paved the way for the euro. In the early years of the euro, any previous shifts into the dollar in anticipation of the euro may reverse themselves as the European Central Bank (ECB) consolidates its credibility and central banks find that they can invest in a deep treasury-bill market in euros.

FIGURE 1

CHANGES IN FORWARD EXCHANGE RATES AGAINST THE MARK
(*in percentages*)

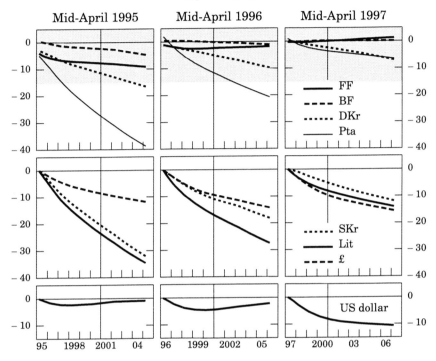

SOURCES: Reuters and BIS calculations.

NOTE: Forward exchange rates are derived from differentials on one-year eurodeposit interest rates and, for longer horizons, on interest-rate swap (midpoint) yields. The currencies of France (FF), Belgium (BF), Denmark (DKr), and Spain (Pta) are plotted relative to their respective central rates; those of Sweden (SKr), Italy (Lit), and the United Kingdom (£) are plotted relative to their spot rates. The lira (Lit) reentered the ERM on November 25, 1996.

Finally, the essay argues against the widespread view that the euro will strengthen secularly against the dollar in the approach to the steady state, owing to large, one-way portfolio shifts into the euro. In fact, given that international borrowers have denominated little of their debt in European currencies, shifts of these liabilities are at least as plausible as the much-discussed asset shifts. Such liability shifts would work against a trend appreciation of the euro against the dollar.

With respect to the volatility of the dollar's exchange rate, any sudden disturbance to the sanguine market outlook for monetary union carries the potential for sharp movements in the dollar/mark rate. In the steady state, the presumption that the ECB will place less weight on the exchange rate than its predecessors must be balanced against the prospect of the more stable transatlantic interest-rate differentials that will result from the broader domain of policymaking in Europe. In any case, monetary union can be expected to raise the volatility to the *effective* dollar, owing to the uniformity of exchange-rate change against a large European trading bloc; any increase in dollar/euro volatility over dollar/mark volatility will only accentuate this tendency.

Framework and Toolkit

To advance the analysis of the dollar/euro exchange rate, I set out a framework for addressing the problem, unpack a useful toolkit, and consider some of the forces bearing on the dollar. The direction of these forces affords some insight into tendencies of both the level and the volatility of the dollar/euro rate.

The responses of three classes of portfolio managers are considered—official reserve-asset managers, private asset managers, and public and private liability managers—during (at least) three stages of monetary union—the period before the irrevocable fixing of conversion rates between existing European currencies and the euro, the period before the ECB has consolidated its credibility, and the steady state beyond union. Monetary union is itself a threefold joint event: it eliminates exchange risk, creates much broader financial markets, and introduces a new central bank with credible antecedents but no independent reputation. Such a mixture, with three actors, three stages, and three transformations, leaves plenty of room for reasonable disagreement.

To help assess what the euro might mean for the dollar, I open a two-drawer toolkit. First, I treat the determination of the exchange rate as a price that balances the demand for, and supply of, financial assets denominated in different currencies (Branson and Henderson, 1985). These assets are taken to be imperfect substitutes, so that their supplies and demands affect the exchange rate. Still, the quantitative impact of substantial portfolio shifts can be fairly subtle (see Appendix A).

Second, I employ an empirical regularity. The observation, first made in the late 1970s (Brown, 1979), is that when the deutsche mark weakens against the dollar, most other European currencies also fall against the dollar but strengthen a little against the mark. Conversely, when the dollar falls against the mark, it also falls against most other European currencies, but to a lesser extent, so that they fall somewhat against the mark.[2] Figure 2 shows the estimated coefficients from a

[2] Subsequent observations and accounts include Frankel (1986), Giavazzi and Giovannini (1989), Group of Ten (1993), Galati (1997), and Galati and McCauley (1997).

FIGURE 2

Sensitivity to Movements in the Mark against the Dollar

—— Swiss franc	·— — Spanish peseta	····· British pound
·—·— Dutch guilder	·— — Swedish krona	······ Australian dollar
—— French franc	———— Italian lira	———— Canadian dollar

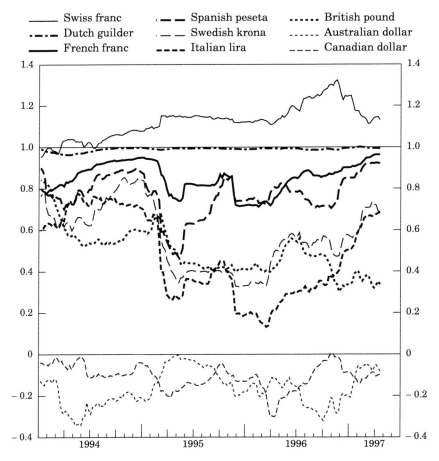

NOTE: Each point represents the weekly average of an estimated elasticity derived as the parameter ß in the regression $\log X/\$_t - X/\$_{t-1} = \alpha + ß(\log DM/\$_t - \log DM/\$_{t-1})$ over the current and previous 125 working days. By definition, the mark/dollar sensitivity to itself is unity, and the sensitivity of the dollar is zero.

regression of the percentage changes in the dollar exchange rates of nine currencies on the percentage changes in the dollar/mark exchange rate, estimated in a sliding window of 125 working days. An observation

---

The Swiss franc, by contrast, tends to amplify the deutsche mark's movements against the dollar, falling against the mark as the mark weakens against the dollar and, conversely, appreciating against the mark as the mark rises against the dollar; see Ettlin (1996).

near one means that a currency moves with the mark, whereas an observation near zero means that it moves with the dollar. Typically, the currencies of Germany's neighbors—and, more recently, the Portuguese escudo and the Spanish peseta—track the mark quite closely, and the British pound, Italian lira, and Swedish krona share half or more of the mark's movements.

Baselines and Caveats

Three caveats are in order at the outset. First, even as profound a development as monetary union will make itself felt against a background of cyclical and secular forces bearing on exchange rates. Any baseline outlook for the dollar's exchange rate against European currencies must reflect the relationship between the business cycle in Europe and in North America and associated interest-rate movements. Thus, the recovery of the dollar in the two years after its trough in the spring of 1995 must be ascribed, first and foremost, to the contrast between the U.S. "hare" and the European "tortoise." By the same token, an upswing in the European economy in 1999 accompanied by a sluggish U.S. economy would make for European currency strength irrespective of monetary union. Similarly, the long-standing U.S. current-account deficit and the consequent cumulative erosion of the U.S. international asset position will continue to weigh on the dollar's value regardless of monetary union. The effects of monetary union discussed in this essay should therefore be understood as deviations from a baseline set by such cyclical and secular factors. In addition, markets may spring surprises that might reinforce or counteract the effects set out here.

Second, this essay musters and relies upon evidence on the currency composition of asset stocks, including official reserves, private assets, and international debts. These stocks will not remain unchanged in the years leading up to monetary union. In particular, the amount and composition of official reserves may change markedly if exchange rates move sharply. Inferences from such cash positions are risky, moreover, because off-balance-sheet positions can transform exposures (Garber, 1996, pp. 9–11).

Finally, the necessary division of the future into distinct periods may prove artificial. If market participants become convinced of a long-term outcome, prices in an intermediate stage will incorporate this conviction, as demonstrated by the narrowing of interest differentials in European bond markets. The force of this last caveat will remain limited, however, as long as market commentary on the euro continues to be diverse and even contradictory.

6

In the discussion that follows, the first organizing principle is time. A separate section for each of the three periods assesses the effect of the behavior of private asset managers and central banks (and global liability managers in the steady state) on the level of the dollar and then takes up the question of exchange-rate volatility in each phase.

2 The Transition Period

The basic question in the months remaining before the introduction of the euro is how portfolio managers will react to the change in currency management in Europe. The ECB will be able to claim a strong lineage, but uncertainties necessarily accompany its approach. Will investors sell European assets and buy dollars?

Private Asset Managers

Market participants accept monetary union as increasingly likely but still ask questions. Which countries will participate? How will parities be determined? What will be the background and character of the ECB's policymaking body? What will be the ECB's objectives and instruments? What will be its foreign-exchange policy? What will be the form of any exchange-rate arrangement (ERM II) with currencies not participating at the outset? Portfolio shifts in response to these uncertainties can affect the level of the dollar.

For private investors *inside* the prospective currency area, the effects of such uncertainties could offset one another in the area as a whole. Although residents of countries with the best inflation records may seek to move assets out of their home currencies, those of countries with less good records may feel reassured and may move assets into their home currencies. To get a net outflow from the euro area would require a situation in which the uncertainties attached to the prospective new currency range well beyond questions about the future behavior of the ECB relative to the recent behavior of its constituent central banks.[3]

Private investors *outside* the euro area, however, might be led by these uncertainties to take defensive positions by shifting their assets into dollars or Swiss francs (at given interest-rate differentials). This possibility gains plausibility from the defensive character of current foreign investment in European fixed-income assets. Holders of bank

---

[3] Something along these lines drew the attention of an official Swiss commission charged with assessing the implication of the euro for the Swiss franc. It considered the possibility that portfolio outflows from the euro area might reach such a volume as to call for a policy of (temporarily) pegging the Swiss franc to the euro (Commission, 1996).

deposits denominated in European currencies show a strong bias toward the "core" European currencies, and the mark in particular, regardless of the residence of the holders of the deposits (Table 2).[4] There appears to be almost as marked a preference in international holdings of securities (Table 3). Recall that French franc deposits have consistently yielded more than mark deposits for over a decade in which the franc has reverted to its central rate after every depreciation. These aggregate portfolios appear to be managed with an eye to preserving capital rather than achieving high returns. The portfolio bias toward the mark thus

TABLE 2

FOREIGN HOLDINGS OF BANK DEPOSITS AT END OF 1996
(in billions of U.S. dollars and percentages)

	Residence of Holder							
Currency	Core EU Country	%	Other EU Country	%	Rest of World	%	Total	%
German mark	98.0	(64)	53.1	(57)	77.7	(51)	228.8	(57)
French franc	18.2	(12)	15.0	(16)	30.0	(20)	63.2	(16)
Dutch guilder	16.6	(11)	7.7	(8)	16.9	(11)	41.2	(10)
Belgian/Lux'bg franc	12.3	(8)	8.9	(10)	16.4	(11)	37.6	(9)
Austrian schilling	1.2	(1)	0.6	(1)	1.5	(1)	3.2	(1)
ECU	7.4	(5)	7.5	(8)	9.9	(6)	24.8	(6)
Subtotal: Core EU currencies	153.7	(100)	92.8	(100)	152.4	(100)	398.8	(100)
Italian lira	15.4	(10)	16.1	(17)	14.1	(9)	45.6	(11)
British pound	17.2	(11)	5.9	(6)	83.8	(55)	106.9	(27)
Other currencies	7.8	(5)	13.0	(14)	9.2	(6)	30.0	(8)
Subtotal: Other EU currencies	40.4	(26)	35.0	(38)	107.1	(70)	182.5	(46)
Total: EU currencies	194.1	(126)	127.8	(138)	259.5	(170)	581.3	(146)
U.S. dollar	109.2	(71)	200.1	(216)	340.6	(224)	649.9	(163)
Swiss franc	16.8	(11)	13.3	(14)	32.8	(22)	62.9	(16)
Japanese yen	12.1	(8)	19.5	(21)	26.4	(17)	58.0	(15)
Grand total	332.1	(216)	360.7	(389)	659.3	(433)	1,352.1	(339)

SOURCE: BIS.
NOTES: Nonbank holdings only; holdings abroad of a given currency by residents of the country of issue are excluded (for example, deutsche mark holdings abroad by German residents are excluded). For Austria, Denmark, Ireland, Finland, Spain, and Sweden, only the cross-border position in domestic currency is available.

[4] For the recent growth of cross-border deposits in Europe, see Monticelli and Papi (1996, chap. 3).

8

TABLE 3

(*in billions of U.S. dollars*)

Currency	In Core EU Banks[a]	In Other EU Banks[b]	In Banks in Rest of World	Total Bank Holdings	Nonresident Holdings of Gov't Bonds	International Securities Outstanding[c]
German mark	144.7	59.2	29.1	233.0	308.5[d]	349.8
French franc	25.4	6.2	7.1	38.7	79.9	168.7
Dutch guilder	8.3	3.6	3.1	15.0	—	95.9
Belgian/Lux'bg franc	8.4	1.4	0.2	10.0	—	56.3
Austrian schilling	0.0	0.0	0.0	0.0	—	3.7
ECU	18.3	13.9	1.1	33.3	—	74.7
Total	205.1	84.3	40.6	330.0	—	749.1

SOURCES: National data and BIS.
[a] Banks in Austria, Belgium, France, Germany, Luxembourg, and the Netherlands.
[b] Banks in Denmark, Finland, Ireland, Italy, Spain, Sweden, and the United Kingdom.
[c] Includes international bonds and medium-term euro notes.
[d] End of June 1996.

suggests an aversion to risk that could lead to net shifts out of core European currencies in the face of the above-mentioned uncertainties.[5] One case in point is that of Japanese life insurers (see Box).

Another way of looking at the distribution of international deposits in European currencies, however, is to interpret it as merely reflecting the role of the deutsche mark as an international currency. That is, rather than reflecting risk aversion, international holdings of marks, particularly bank deposits, may result from nothing more than the close substitutability of the mark with other European currencies and the ease with which it can be transformed into any one of them. On the latter point, not only is dollar/mark trading far larger than the trading of any other European currency against the dollar, the mark is also the interbank vehicle for almost all trading between Continental currencies. When a bank exchanges a customer's French francs for Italian lire, for

[5] The Deutsche Bundesbank (1997) recently drew attention to the foreign holdings of deutsche marks in order to warn that the transition to the euro must be handled with care to ensure that the high degree of confidence in the mark is sustained and passed on to the euro. The Bundesbank measured foreign holdings at DM 1.4 trillion (about $800 billion) at end-1996, excluding trade credits and direct investments in Germany. The Bundesbank (1997, p. 30) characterized the "outstanding international role of the Deutsche Mark [as] . . . undoubtedly a considerable challenge to the planned single European currency—the euro."

CASE STUDY: JAPANESE LIFE INSURERS

Another indication of a strong, albeit recent, bias in private portfolios toward deutsche mark assets is the distribution of the foreign assets of Japanese life insurance companies. I examine the distribution of bond holdings because Japanese insurers' bank deposits in Europe have been minimal (with the exception of Swiss franc deposits from 1995 to 1997). This evidence is worth consulting because there are few reliable breakdowns of the bond holdings of any important class of internationally active institutional investor. These mostly mutual life insurance companies represent the largest single group of institutional investors in the world's largest creditor country, but no claim is made for their representativeness. The earliest detail on their portfolios shows them to have favored higher-interest-rate investments in Europe, that is, the portfolios were strongly tilted away from the deutsche mark in September 1991: they had only 3 percent of their bond portfolio in German bonds and 24 percent in other European bonds (see table below). Against a background of overall shrinkage in the foreign-bond holdings of these institutions, and the increasing weight placed within their foreign-bond holdings on euro-yen bonds (see McCauley and Yeaple, 1994, pp. 19–33), these portfolios seem never to have recovered from the shock of the ERM crises of 1992–93. By September 1995, 7 percent of their foreign-bond portfolio was invested in German bonds, only 3 percent in French bonds, and only 1 percent in ECU bonds.

FOREIGN-BOND HOLDINGS OF JAPANESE LIFE INSURERS
(in percentages)

Currency	1991	1992	1993	1994	1995	1997
Europe	27	23	30	19	12	11
German mark	3	6	11	6	7	5
French franc	9	7	12	9	3	1
ECU	6	4	2	2	1	1
British pound	5	3	4	1	1	3
Spanish peseta	1	1	0	0	0	0
Other	3	2	1	0	0	1
Dollar bloc	63	69	61	52	43	58
U.S.	32	35	38	39	37	54
Canadian	21	24	17	8	5	3
Australian	10	10	7	5	1	1
Other[a]	11	9	8	30	45	31
Total (¥ trillion)	11.5	10.6	7.9	5.1	6.5	13.2
Memorandum: Ratio of German bonds to total German, French, and ECU bonds	*0.15*	*0.30*	*0.44*	*0.30*	*0.63*	*0.76*

SOURCE: Koo, "Japan and International Capital Flows," 1992–1996, and personal communication for 1997 data.

NOTE: Data are for September, except for 1997, when they are for March. Figures are rounded and may not sum to 100.

[a] Mostly euro-yen bonds.

example, it will typically transact a pair of exchanges in the interbank market: marks against lire and francs against marks. Of an estimated $150 billion in transactions among European Union (EU) currencies in April 1995 (shown with double-counting in Table 4 as $300 billion), the deutsche mark was on one side of the transaction in over $140 billion.[6]

Under these conditions, a European corporate treasury trying to minimize its transactions costs while reducing its working capital would centralize its bank deposits in European currencies in deutsche mark accounts. On this reading of the evidence, the distribution of asset stocks across currencies in Table 2 reflects the manner in which market participants have already exploited the mark's vehicle property to economize on their holdings of bank deposits in different European currencies. An important implication is that after monetary union, these international bank deposits might not decline as one might imagine.[7] That is, to the extent that deutsche mark deposits are already held to make payments at one remove in either Dutch guilders or French francs, then the arrival of the euro may not much shrink the demand for the participating currencies. I return to this point in the next section.

What does the evidence show? To some analysts, the prospective movement of private investors out of the deutsche mark is already a reality. A Swiss commission (Commission, 1996, p. 2) examining Swiss policy options in the face of monetary union claimed:

> The fear that the future single currency does not have the quality of the DM or other currencies belonging to the DM-group, induces investors to exchange these currencies, in particular the DM, into other strong international currencies, among others into the Swiss franc. As a result, there are strong tendencies for the Swiss franc to increase in value.

A variant is the observation that deutsche mark bonds, especially those maturing in the next century, yield a high interest rate because of uncertainty regarding the euro. The claimed effect of such shifts has been summarized with the provocative statement that "the euro . . . is already . . . a weak currency" (Persaud, 1996, p. 3). Events that make the euro more or less likely are thus seen to weaken or strengthen the mark against the dollar.

---

[6] Here and throughout, "billion" equals one thousand million.

[7] Baumol's (1952) argument that the transactions demand for money rises with the square root of spending, applied to a variety of currencies that become one currency, implies that transactions bank balances will decline. See Honohan (1984) for the opposite case, when sterling bifurcated into the British pound and the Irish punt.

TABLE 4

European Monetary Union and Foreign-Exchange Turnover in April 1995
(in billions of U.S. dollars and percentages)

Currency	Actual Turnover against					Hypothetical, with Monetary Union (total less all EMS)[c]	%
	Dollar[a]	Mark[a]	All EMS[b]	Total[a]	%		
U.S. dollar	—	365	714	1,313	84%	1,313	92%
EU currencies/euro[d]	714	140	*300*	1,099	70%	*799*	*56%*
German mark	365	—	140	584		*(443)*	
French franc	72	50	*53*	127		*(74)*	
Dutch guilder	*18*	7	*9*	27		*(18)*	
Belgian/Lux'bg franc	*20*	8	*9*	29		*(20)*	
Austrian schilling	*5*	3	*3*	8		*(5)*	
ECU	25	10	*11*	36		*(25)*	
Irish punt	*2*	0	*1*	3		*(2)*	
Finnish markka	*3*	2	*2*	5		*(3)*	
Spanish peseta	25	8	*8*	*33*		*(25)*	
Portuguese escudo	*2*	1	*2*	4		*(2)*	
Italian lira	39	9	*10*	49		*(39)*	
Danish krone	*17*	5	*6*	23		*(17)*	
Swedish krona	*15*	9	*10*	26		*(15)*	
British pound	103	29	*32*	140		*(108)*	
Greek drachma	*2*	1	*2*	4		*(2)*	
Japanese yen	329	33		371	24%	371	26%
Swiss franc	86	26		116		116	
Canadian dollar	49	1		50		50	
Australian dollar	39			40		40	
Emerging currencies	23			25		25	
Hong Kong dollar	14			15		15	
Singapore dollar	5			6		6	
South African rand	4			4		4	
Other reporting countries and unallocated	71	18		130		130	
Grand total (÷ 2)	1,313	584	1,099	1,572	100%	*1,422*	100%

SOURCES: BIS, *Central Bank Survey 1995*, Consensus Economics, *Consensus Forecasts*, August 1997, and author's calculations.

NOTE: Because the table reports the turnover (net of local interdealer double-counting) for which a given currency appears on one side of a transaction, each transaction is counted twice. The grand total is therefore divided by two and set to 100 percent. Estimates are shown in italics; the contribution of EU currencies to euro turnover is shown in parentheses. Components are rounded and may not sum to totals.

[a] Decompositions for EU currencies other than the mark, franc, ECU, and pound are estimated using each currency's local-currency trading as a proportion of such trading for all other EMS currencies.

[b] Estimated EMS totals for currencies other than the French franc or British pound are calculated as the currency total *less* that currency's trading against the dollar (local trading against other currencies is negligible). The French franc (or British pound) EMS total is estimated as the total *less* the sum of its trading against the dollar, against the yen in Tokyo, against the Swiss franc in Zurich, and against the yen, Swiss franc, Canadian dollar, and Australian dollar in Paris (or London).

[c] Because some intra-EMS transactions using the U.S. dollar as a vehicle will disappear under monetary union, the currency shares shown overstate the importance of the euro, understate the importance of the yen, and correctly represent the importance of the dollar.

[d] EU currencies (excluding the ECU) are ordered according to poll respondents' views on the probability of countries joining monetary union at the outset (Consensus Economics, *Consensus Forecasts*, 1997).

All of these claims can be and have been disputed. Thus, the Bundesbank (1997, p. 30) notes that "the available data on the currency structure of international assets (even when interpreted with caution) argue against the supposition of 'a flight out of the Deutsche Mark.'" Indeed, Table 2 was originally assembled with end-1995 data, which were not very different from the end-1996 data. Quite apart from any flight from the mark, non-German European investors may shift their marks into Swiss francs to balance the risk of their dollar holdings (Appendix B). As for the effect of the prospect of monetary union on German bond yields, an International Monetary Fund (IMF) study looked in vain at scores of monetary union events for evidence of systematic effects on German and other European bond yields (Zettelmeyer, 1997).[8] Moreover, a variety of analysts marshaled the evidence to suggest that the slope of the German yield curve was no steeper than one would expect, given the unprecedentedly low short-term rates and the historical relation between those rates and the slope of the yield curve (King, 1996, p. 12). As for the connection between measures of the likelihood of monetary union (Persaud, 1996) and the dollar/mark exchange rate, recall the long-standing association of a strong dollar and strong European currencies against the mark. Although conceding grounds for both readings, the relation is perhaps better read from left to right than from right to left. Brighter prospects for broad monetary union may have tended to strengthen the dollar, but a cyclically strong dollar has surely paved the way to monetary union.

Central Banks

The question of how the prospect and introduction of the euro might affect central banks' management of their official reserves has attracted a great deal of market comment (see, in chronological order, O'Neill, Bevan, and Brookes, 1996; Keating, 1996; Ruskin, 1996; Owens, 1996; Persaud and Dambassinas, 1996; Brookes, 1996; Parsons, 1996; Golden, 1996; Adler and Chang, 1996; Lipsky et al., 1996; Bulchandani, 1997;

---

[8] But one's confidence in the null finding is undermined by the coding of the events around September 20, 1995, as "ambiguous," when the clearly dominant event was official German questioning of the policy fitness of certain aspiring countries for monetary union; see BIS (1996b, pp. 101, 103). Zettelmeyer measures that day's effect on bond yields as a decline in German rates of 6 basis points and a rise in Italian rates of 10 basis points. More recently, the compromise at the Amsterdam intergovernmental conference, accommodating the new French government's requirements to some extent, saw the German bond yields rise, Italian bond yields fall, and the mark slip against the dollar.

13

Deutsch, 1997; Alzola, 1997; and Hoffman and Schröder, 1997). It needs
to be stressed at the outset that official reserves at the end of 1996, even
after a year when they grew by a record amount—$200 billion at constant
exchange rates to a stock of $1.5 trillion (BIS, 1997b, p. 83)—represent
only a fraction of the private portfolios that may react to the introduction
of the euro.[9]

Some central banks outside the Group of Ten (G–10) could also
adopt a defensive strategy in the run-up to monetary union. With $118
billion in deutsche mark reserves out of core European reserves of
$132 billion at end-1996, the central banks in nonindustrial countries
show a similar bias toward the deutsche mark (Table 5).[10] If this
concentration of holdings reflects risk aversion, then central-bank

TABLE 5

COMPOSITION OF NONINDUSTRIAL-COUNTRY RESERVES AT END OF 1996
(*in billions of U.S. dollars and percentages*)

Currency	All Developing Countries	%	of which: Taiwan	%	Eastern Europe	%	Total	%	Global Total	%
U.S. dollar	531.9	(71.5)	50.6	(57.5)	34.1	(51.0)	566.0	(69.8)	1,041.5	(68.6)
Japanese yen	60.8	(8.2)	13.0	(14.8)	0.0	(0.0)	60.8	(7.5)	105.3	(6.9)
Core EU	101.0	(13.6)	20.3	(23.1)	31.2	(46.7)	132.2	(16.3)	303.6	(20.0)
German mark	87.1	(11.7)	20.3	(23.1)	30.5	(45.6)	117.6	(14.5)	246.1	(16.2)
French franc	10.1	(1.4)	0.0	(0.0)	0.7	(1.1)	10.8	(1.3)	23.2	(1.5)
Dutch guilder	3.8	(0.5)	0.0	(0.0)	0.0	(0.0)	3.8	(0.5)	5.1	(0.3)
British pound	36.4	(4.9)	0.0	(0.0)	0.9	(1.3)	37.3	(4.6)	52.1	(3.4)
Swiss franc	13.9	(1.9)	4.0	(4.6)	0.7	(1.1)	14.6	(1.8)	15.4	(1.0)
Total	744.0	(100.0)	88.0	(100.0)	67.0	(100.0)	810.9	(100.0)	1,517.8	(100.0)

SOURCES: Hong Kong Monetary Authority, *Annual Report 1996*; Taiwan authorities; U.S. Treasury,
Treasury Bulletin, March 1997, table IFS-2; IMF, and BIS estimates.

NOTES: Developing countries include Hong Kong and Taiwan. Taiwan's disclosed dollar share as
of April 1996 is applied to holdings at the end of 1996; disclosed shares of yen, marks, and Swiss
francs as of August 1995 are reduced proportionately to accommodate the (higher) dollar share of
April 1996. Core EU currencies include holdings of private ECUs. Dollar reserves of developing
countries are reduced by the current value of the Brady bond collateral held at the Federal Reserve
Bank of New York and by advance payments for U.S. military exports as reported in the *Treasury
Bulletin*. The reserve composition of Eastern European countries is estimated. The global total
includes industrial countries.

[9] For the contrast in the growth of official reserves and private international assets over
a generation, see Icard (1996, p. 180).

[10] Contrary to Garber's (1996, p. 6) claim that "all studies of the currency composition
of foreign exchange [reserves] depend on the data contained in the IMF's *Annual
Reports*," these data include the reported or estimated reserve compositions of Taiwan,
Hong Kong, and Eastern Europe.

14

reserve managers might readily justify shifts into the dollar, the yen, or the Swiss franc as a way of avoiding uncertainties.[11] In this respect, these official portfolio managers may resemble private investors.

A review of European central-bank reserve management (Appendix C) suggests that the central banks will probably not supply a substantial net sum of marks to the foreign-exchange market in preparation for the pooling of their reserves at the ECB. Some European central banks may wish to sustain their international reserve holdings by converting marks into dollars in the approach to the creation of the ECB, but others may be happy to lighten their reserve holdings by letting their mark assets become euro assets. The prospect of pooling ECU 50 billion of reserves with the ECB, as required by the Maastricht Treaty, does not seem likely to force any rebalancing of reserves toward the dollar. Moreover, by June 1997, no European government seemed to

FIGURE 3

THE NOMINAL EFFECTIVE DOLLAR EXCHANGE RATE AND EMS REALIGNMENTS
(*index, week of realignment = 100*)

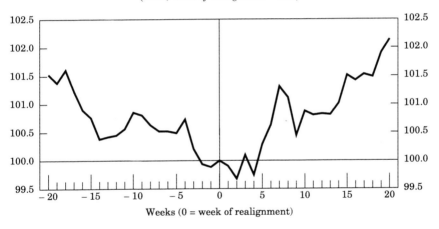

Weeks (0 = week of realignment)

NOTE: The figure shows the nominal effective dollar rates calculated by the Federal Reserve as averages for the twenty weeks before and after the eighteen EMS realignment dates; the averages are normalized at 100 at the times of the realignments, which were on September 24 and November 30, 1979, March 23 and October 5, 1981, February 22 and June 14, 1982, March 22, 1983, July 22, 1985, April 7 and August 4, 1986, January 12, 1987, January 8, 1990, September 14 and November 23, 1992, February 1, May 14, and August 2, 1993, and March 6, 1995. September 17, 1992, the date of the floating of the pound and lira, is not included.

[11] If most of the nonindustrial-country currencies trade predominantly against the dollar, the transaction motive for the concentration of deutsche mark holdings, as sketched above for private investors, would seem not to apply here.

15

FIGURE 4

TEN-YEAR YIELD DIFFERENTIALS AND EUROPEAN EXCHANGE RATES

(*at end of month*)

Left-hand scale (in percentage points):[a]
——— Swap rate
•••••• Benchmark government yield

Right-hand scales (against the mark):[b]
– – – Exchange rate
– – – ERM central rate

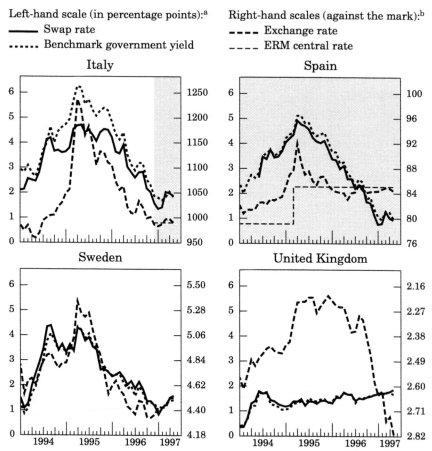

SOURCES: Reuters, Datastream, and BIS.

NOTE: Shaded areas denote ERM membership.

[a] Domestic *less* German rate.

[b] Scaled to show a 35 percent range of variation; for the United Kingdom, mark/pound (inverted scale). A decline indicates an appreciation of the domestic currency.

regard the exchange rate of the dollar as a problem, and there appeared to be no policy interest in selling marks for dollars.[12]

_____

[12] There was considerable discussion in France about the proper exchange rate of the dollar in late 1996 and early 1997. Although the new Socialist government in France had

A further consideration is that a weak dollar has often accompanied strains in European exchange rates that have resulted in realignments (Figure 3). But if, as considered above, the dollar benefits from defensive portfolio shifts in the run-up to monetary union, the odds rise for a prolonged virtuous circle of strong European cross rates against the deutsche mark and convergent European interest rates (Figure 4). Aware of the possibility of this virtuous circle, and perhaps also anticipating a need to offset the cumulative effect of Maastricht-timed fiscal tightening in Europe, market participants seem to expect little resistance among European policymakers to a stronger dollar in this period. Even when the Bundesbank raised short-term interest rates in the fall of 1997, citing the dangers of import-price inflation, market participants interpreted the move less as an attempt to reverse the prior decline than as insurance against further large movements in the same direction.

Volatility

With respect to the volatility of the dollar/mark exchange rate during the transition period, should strains arise in the process of monetary union, these could not only weaken the dollar but also increase its volatility. The events of mid-September 1995, when doubts about which European countries would qualify for monetary union came to center stage, serve as an example. Although increased attention to policy performance tended to weaken European currencies against the mark, the dollar also plunged 6 pfennigs (4 percent) on September 21 and 22 (Figure 5). Moreover, option prices suggested that expectations of the dollar's value one month ahead became more diffuse, and the odds of a sharp change—for example, of 5 percent or more—shifted from dollar strengthening to dollar weakening (See Figure 6 and McCauley and Melick, 1996a, 1996b). European events can move the dollar.[13]

---

made a more competitive franc vis-à-vis the dollar one of its conditions for supporting monetary union (along with an "economic government for Europe," a "solidarity and growth pact," and inclusion of Spain and Italy in the first wave of participants in monetary union), the finance minister told a press conference that the "dollar has moved in such a way that the problem is not topical, at least for the moment" (quoted in "French govt has 'no problem' with dlr level — minister," Reuters, June 16, 1997 [16:39]).

[13] The generality of such European influences on the dollar has been questioned. Johnson, (1994, p. 8) found no systematic relation between fairly long periods of high and low volatility in the French franc/deutsche mark exchange rate, on the one hand, and the volatility of the ECU/dollar exchange rate, on the other. Still, the "September 1992 episode of extreme instability in the Exchange Rate Mechanism (ERM) suggests that during shorter intervals, spillover to the dollar from ERM volatility may be present."

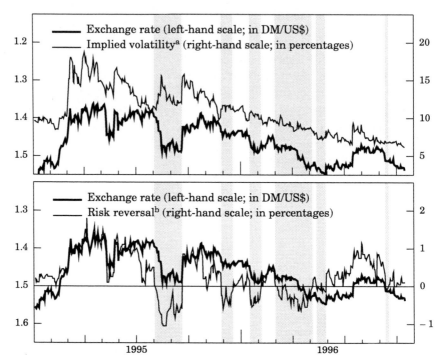

FIGURE 5

THE MARK AGAINST THE DOLLAR

SOURCES: National Westminster Bank and BIS.
[a] One month at the money.
[b] A positive (negative) value indicates a bias toward deutsche mark (dollar) strength. The shaded areas represent periods in which risk reversals favor the dollar.

If unguarded commentary two and a half years before the selection of participants in the monetary union can move intra-European exchange rates and dollar rates, what will be the consequences of an actual decision that a country will not participate in the union? Saccomanni (1996, p. 390) suggests that "the currencies of non-participating countries may be subject to strong downward pressures, irrespective of the degree of divergence of their economies from the Treaty criteria, just because of the very decision of not having been included in the euro" (see also Arrowsmith and Taylor, 1996, pp. 20–21, and De Grauwe, 1996b, p. 21). The events of February–March 1997, when market participants received reports that a mooted deal would leave Italy out of the union initially but with the strong prospect of its joining in a year or two, suggest that nonparticipation itself might not make for an

FIGURE 6

THE PROBABILITY DISTRIBUTION OF THE MARK AGAINST THE DOLLAR
(*average density in period*)

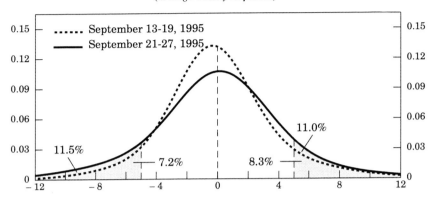

SOURCES: National Westminster Bank, BIS, and BIS calculations.

NOTE: Percentage deviation from the forward rate (vertical lines drawn at rate and at 5 percent above and below the rate); positive values indicate dollar appreciation.

exchange-rate shock. Rather, an overall delay not convincingly limited in time is generally judged to be the scenario that would push up the mark abruptly, not least against the dollar (King, 1996; Davies, 1997; but see also Clarke and Parry, 1997).

Summary

The assessment of the risk of a shift by private portfolio managers in the run-up to the introduction of the euro depends on one's interpretation of the bias toward the mark in those portfolios. If the heavy weight attached to deutsche mark holdings—also noticeable in the reserve holdings of nonindustrial countries—signals risk avoidance, then the coming months, with their many uncertainties, may see these funds shifted into the Swiss franc, the dollar, or the yen. If the heavy weight, particularly in short-term portfolios, reflects, instead, the transaction-cost advantage of holding the mark as a vehicle currency for transactions across Europe, then near-term portfolio shifts seem less likely. Even less likely is any substantial shift by European official reserve managers. As for the volatility of exchange rates, the very strength of the conviction of a broad monetary union implies that any serious doubts could give rise to instability among exchange rates, including the dollar/mark rate.[14]

---

[14] For the linkage of the strong dollar to subdued volatility, see BIS (1997b, p. 81).

3 The Early Years of the ECB

The formation of the ECB and the introduction of the euro should relieve some of the uncertainties cited above. As time goes by, financial-market participants as well as wage and price setters will discern the ECB's character. In this second phase, extending from the inception of the euro at least until the disappearance of the constituent national currencies (scheduled for 2002), the ECB will also give evidence of its exchange-rate policy. Much of the discussion of this period centers on whether the ECB will pursue a tough interest-rate policy or will react with unusual vigor to a weakening of the euro against the dollar. At the same time, other uncertainties may arise: interest rates and exchange rates might show volatility as the ECB and market participants grope for a common understanding of policy targets and instruments and their nuances.

Private Asset Managers

Private asset managers might shift funds into the euro upon demonstration of, or indeed in anticipation of, a firm-interest-rate and strong-currency policy on the part of the ECB. The European Commission (1997b, p. 9) casts doubt on "an often heard argument . . . that the ECB would attempt to establish early counter inflation credibility by adopting a tight monetary policy stance" on the grounds that "there is . . . no reason to assume that the Bank will not enjoy counter inflation credibility from the outset." The Bundesbank's chief economist dismissed as a "nice idea" the notion that the ECB would, despite high European unemployment, pursue a particularly restrictive policy at the outset.[15] It will probably be very difficult even after the fact to know whether the ECB has shown a bias toward firm rates.[16] With respect to exchange-rate policy, one can debate how much European monetary policy will respond to exchange-rate movements in the steady state, but several considerations suggest that the ECB might put considerable weight on the exchange rate in its early years. Were the euro to weaken during this period, not only financial-market participants but also domestic wage and price setters would look to the ECB's reaction for evidence bearing on its credibility. Put another way, the first "referen-

---

[15] Otmar Issing, speaking before the European Summer Institute (quoted in Stüdemann, 1997).

[16] One approach would be to look for deviations from a Taylor rule for ECB policy; see Clarida, Gali, and Gertler (1997).

dum" on the ECB could be conducted in the foreign-exchange market, and the authorities might thus respond vigorously, whatever the cyclical circumstances.[17]

A particular dilemma could arise for the new directors of the ECB if the consolidation of credibility were to take on importance against the background of a strong U.S. economy and a weak European economy. If some European countries were not to join monetary union from the outset but were to enter an ERM II, however, dollar weakness could also pose challenges. The tendency for most European currencies to decline against the deutsche mark when the dollar does so could continue, with ERM II currencies weakening against the euro when the dollar weakens. Any association of strains in the ERM II with dollar weakness against the euro could put dollar weakness on the agenda at the ECB. But the salience of dollar weakness would depend on the design of ERM II, especially on its fluctuation margins and related intervention obligations (Saccomanni, 1996).

Central Banks

The introduction of the euro will make it easier for central banks to invest in the world's second-largest reserve currency. Until recently, the Bundesbank's opposition to short-term finance has kept the German finance ministry from floating part of its debt as treasury bills. As a result, many risk-averse central banks were denied their natural investing habitat of short-term government bills and, with some discomfort, had to deposit their deutsche mark reserves with banks. Some central banks used bond futures to shorten the duration on holdings of German government bonds or used currency forwards to convert U.S. Treasury bills into synthetic deutsche mark treasury bills. But far from all central banks are able and willing to employ such strategies.

Whatever the debt-management policy of the German government, the other triple-A governments in the euro area will ensure a supply of euro-denominated treasury bills that is ample enough to satisfy all central-bank demands. Central banks probably should not be expected to reallocate their portfolios abruptly in January 1999, in response to this new menu item in the world's second-largest reserve currency, but it could make it easier for central banks, particularly in emerging markets, to diversify thereafter into the euro.

---

[17] Masson and Turtelboom (1997) and Funke and Kennedy (1997) speak of the privileged policy position that the exchange rate might occupy in the euro's early days.

Volatility

In the early days of the ECB, market participants will have to discover not only the bank's objectives, but also the way in which it intends to use its policy instruments to achieve those objectives. Participants will need time to learn to read the nuances of the ECB's operations. The challenge of clearly and simultaneously signaling ECB intentions to market participants, given the aim of operating in a number of national markets with different structures, could make for more volatile money markets and exchange markets.

A reasonable hunch is that the money-market operations by the ECB need not impart much volatility to money or foreign-exchange markets if European policymakers value stability. Whatever the importance placed on one or more monetary aggregates as an intermediate target, the Bundesbank has, since the bond-market turbulence of 1994, relied heavily on the fixed-rate tender for its operations. Rather than putting out a fixed quantity of reserves and letting the price reflect demand pressures, the fixed-rate tender allows quantities to adjust. If, in the future, repurchase transactions are to be conducted simultaneously by a number of national central banks, the argument for fixing the rate could prove very convincing.

One might hope that any monetary implications of the consolidation of internationally held bank deposits denominated in a number of European currencies will be anticipated, even if not measured exactly, ahead of time and will be handled without destabilizing European money markets and the foreign-exchange market. Again, balances in deutsche marks, French francs, Dutch guilders, and so on needed to meet payments in those specific currencies will, to some extent, become unnecessarily large under the single currency. Thus, adding up all the current payment flows in n currencies will render transactions balances redundant. Putting aside the question of whether the concentration of deposits in the mark implies that the consolidation has already occurred to a substantial extent, there remains the question of the monetary implications of any economizing on these balances. In particular, it is not clear that these balances entail much of a demand for base money. For instance, possibly reservable foreign holdings of deutsche mark bank deposits in Germany are much smaller than foreign holdings of deutsche mark bank deposits in Luxembourg, London, and elsewhere abroad.[18] Again, a monetary policy that fixes

---

[18] More precisely, nonresident nonbank holdings of marks in Germany, which may require the holding of reserves, are smaller than the holdings of marks outside Germany

the repurchase rate should permit adjustment in these balances without turmoil in the money market.

More difficult might be the market's reading of foreign-exchange policy per se. It is particularly difficult to judge ahead of time how national differences in the importance attached to exchange-rate stability will work out in practice. If the ECB's directors are not of one mind on this matter, market expectations could be quite volatile. There is the question, moreover, of the role of the political authorities in foreign-exchange-rate policy.

Kenen (1995, p. 123) has argued, in addition, that an ECB single-mindedly focused on domestic stability might eschew international coordination to limit dollar/euro exchange-rate volatility:

> The ECB will want to earn credibility by proving its ability to maintain price stability. Hence it may resist EC involvement in any attempt at exchange rate management by the G–7 countries, especially if it were seen to require heavy intervention on the foreign exchange market.

Volatility in the early years of the ECB might also arise if some countries do not join monetary union in the first round. Both De Grauwe (1996b, p. 21; 1997) and Spaventa (1996, p. 54) predict higher volatility between the euro and the excluded currencies, although Spaventa limits his prediction to the case in which an effective ERM II is not put in place. It is hard to imagine that intra-European volatility would not induce volatility in the dollar/euro exchange rate.

Summary

The early years of the ECB may see portfolio reflows toward the euro. Private market participants may anticipate a tilt toward a firmer interest-rate policy and a bias against euro depreciation during a period in which the ECB is consolidating its credibility. Central banks will enjoy in short order the opportunity to invest in a liquid market for high-quality treasury bills denominated in euro. Monetary-policy operations conducted in a variety of markets may of necessity adopt a transparent procedure that avoids leaving private market participants guessing at the ECB's intentions, with implications for money-market volatility and knock-on effects in the bond market and foreign-exchange market. Still, the inevitable process of defining the new central bank's foreign-exchange policy could prove a source of market volatility.

---

by non-German resident nonbanks ($96 billion as compared to $133 billion); see BIS (1997a, pp. 11, 13, and table A.5.1).

4 Toward the Steady State

The steady-state role of the euro in relation to the dollar and yen is a subject that attracts more attention than it produces consensus. In the early 1970s, at the beginning of the period of general floating, Triffin (1973, p. 78) foresaw that the "Community's unit of account would also be likely to be used more and more, in lieu of the Eurodollar, in private lending and borrowing operations." A generation later, however, Kindleberger (1996, pp. 187–188) noted that "the surprise in this history is that . . . there was no general revulsion against lending in depreciating dollars. . . . The world stayed with the dollar as a limping standard faute de mieux."[19] The "640 billion euro" question is whether offering a heavy-weight alternative to the "limping standard" will attract a large net portfolio shift from the dollar.

In the steady state, four slowly evolving developments could bear on the level and volatility of the dollar. First, the size of the euro area could lead to a wider use of the euro as an anchor for the exchange rates of smaller countries. Second, the increase in the liquidity of the financial markets denominated in euros could affect the behavior of private portfolio managers. Many analysts stop at this point and conclude that the euro will attract a large net portfolio shift from the dollar. But more anchoring to the euro and more liquid euro financial markets could alter the choice of currency denomination made by debt managers, a third development, which is discussed below. Fourth, unified European exchange rates could increase *effective* dollar volatility even if the dollar/euro rate were no more volatile than the historical dollar/mark rate. Moreover, a possible waning of concern about exchange-rate movements in European policymaking could raise the volatility of the dollar/euro rate relative to the historical dollar/mark rate.

The Euro as an Anchor Currency

Some observers imagine that the euro, backed by the world's largest single economy, could provide an anchor for a broad range of countries outside the euro area proper. With currencies linked to the euro, private traders might increasingly denominate their transactions in the euro, a practice that would lead them to hold working balances in euros and would ultimately reinforce any tendency for private and

---

[19] Or as de Boissieu (1996, p. 130) puts it: "Since the end of the 1960s . . . the dollar has been challenged without being replaced."

official portfolios to shift into the euro. Let us consider the euro as an anchor currency, starting with the countries nearest to the prospective euro area and working outward from there.

The linkage of Central and Eastern European currencies to the euro looks likely to many observers (Alogoskoufis and Portes, 1992, pp. 277–278; Arrowsmith and Taylor, 1996, p. 21; Berrigan and Carré, 1997; Frenkel and Goldstein, 1997). Already, daily movements of the Hungarian forint, Polish zloty, and Czech koruna against the dollar share about half of the deutsche mark's movement (Figure 7). Similarly, official reserves and foreign debts appear to be divided roughly half-and-half between the two largest reserve currencies. Close trade and investment links between Eastern and Western Europe suggest the appropriateness of a euro anchor (Bénassy-Quéré, 1996b, pp. 42–44). Some observers suggest that the introduction of the euro and foresee-able progress on EU accession by Central European countries could lead to the pegging of the forint, zloty, Czech koruna, and Slovak koruna to the euro, perhaps as part of some ERM II (Backé and Lindner, 1996). The Czech authorities have indicated that they plan to peg the koruna to the euro when it comes into existence (Thorpe et al., 1997, p. 179).[20] Moreover, in June 1997, the Bulgarian authorities, struggling to stabilize the lev, chose to peg it to the mark (at 1,000 to 1, making life easy for Italian tourists in Sofia). Continuation of this trend would replace a zone of hybrid currency pegs in Central Europe with a euro zone (Table 6).

This development could expose the trade between the broad euro area and the successor states of the Soviet Union to movements of the dollar/euro exchange rate. Under these circumstances, the dollar orientation of the ruble might come into question. One can imagine the ruble following the path of the zloty, which overcame very high inflation with the help of a dollar peg but was then switched to a hybrid peg in May 1991 (Radzyner and Riesinger, 1996; Koch, 1997), and may eventually be pegged to the euro. Although trade with the euro area would tend to induce the Russian authorities to peg the ruble to the euro, inertia, trade with Asia and the Americas, and the importance of Russia's commodity exports would all work to keep the ruble anchored to the dollar. Inertia favors the dollar because the ruble is currently managed against the dollar and tens of millions of hundred-

---

[20] Unsurprisingly, the Estonian kroon, currently worth 12.5 pfennig, is to be fixed to the euro; see Thornhill, 1997.

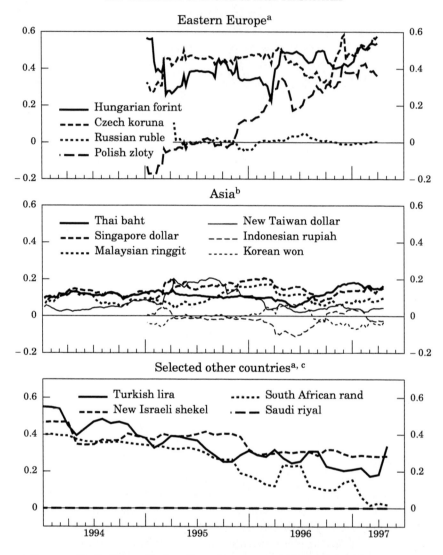

FIGURE 7

THE GEOGRAPHY OF EXCHANGE-RATE SENSITIVITIES

Eastern Europe[a]

Hungarian forint
Czech koruna
Russian ruble
Polish zloty

Asia[b]

Thai baht — New Taiwan dollar
Singapore dollar — Indonesian rupiah
Malaysian ringgit — Korean won

Selected other countries[a, c]

Turkish lira — South African rand
New Israeli shekel — Saudi riyal

SOURCES: Bank of Japan, Bankers Trust, Datastream, and International Monetary Fund.

[a] Sensitivity to movements in the mark against the dollar (see Figure 2, note).

[b] Sensitivity to movements in the yen against the dollar (by definition, the yen/dollar sensitivity to itself is unity).

[c] Over the current and previous thirty-six months.

TABLE 6

EXCHANGE-RATE REGIMES AND POLICIES IN CENTRAL EUROPE

Country	Regime	Basket	Fluctuation Bands	Stability
Bulgaria	Currency board	DM	—	Started July 1, '97
Czech Republic	Managed float (peg from Jan. '91 to May '97)	DM (45% DM, 31% $, 12% Sch, 7% SF, 4% £ from Jan. '91 to May '93; 65% DM, 35% $ until May '97)	None (±0.5% from Jan. '91 to Feb. '96; ±7.5% until May '97)	Peg successfully attacked May '97
Hungary	Crawling peg (adjustable peg before March '95)	70% DM, 30% $ ('91 to July '93: 50% ECU, 50% $; until Aug. '94: 50% DM, 50% $; until Jan. '97: 70% ECU, 30% $)	±2.25%	1.4% devaluation in Jan. '95; 2% in Feb. '95; 9% in March '95; then automatic monthly devaluation rate of 1.9% until June '95; 1.3% until Dec. '95; 1.2% in '96; 1.1% in '97
Poland	Crawling peg ($ peg from Jan. '90 to May '91)	45% $, 35% DM 10% £, 5% FF, 5% SF	±7% (±0.5% until March '95; ±2% until May '95)	14% devaluation in May '91, 11% in Feb. '92, 7% in Aug. '93; automatic monthly devaluation of 1.8% from Oct. '91 to Aug. '93, 1.6% until Sep. '94, 1.5% until Nov. '94, 1.4% until Feb '95, 1.2% until Jan. '96, 1% since; in addition, 6% revaluation in Dec. '95
Slovak Republic	Fixed peg	60% DM, 40% $ since July '94	±5% (±1.5% until Dec. '95; ±3% until July '96)	Stable against the basket since 10% devaluation in July '93
Slovenia	Managed float	—	—	9% depreciation against ECU between Jan. '95 and Oct. '96

SOURCES: Backé and Lindner, "European Monetary Union," 1996; Radzyner and Riesinger, "Exchange Rate Policy in Transition," 1996; BIS, *Handbook on Central Banks*, 1997c, extended and updated by the author.

dollar bills circulate in Russia. Trade with Asia and the Americas, presumably conducted in dollars, could prove more dynamic than trade with Europe if rapid Asian growth persists and the EU agricultural policy proves inhospitable to imports from the east.

The effective dollar anchoring of commodity prices helps to sustain the dollar orientation of Russian and other commodity producers. Dollar commodity prices are usually more stable than commodity prices expressed in marks, so that Russian oil and gold exports tend to yield a more stable stream of rubles with a dollar anchor for the currency.[21] Certainly, the dollar price of gold shows much less sensitivity to movements in the dollar/mark rate than it did a decade and a half ago (Figure 8),[22] perhaps because the balance of private demand for gold has tipped from European investors to nouveaux riches in dollar-linked Asia (Murray, Klapwijk, le Roux, and Walker, 1997, pp. 44–45). More generally, if the sensitivity of commodity prices to the dollar's exchange rate depends on the fraction of demand outside the dollar area (Dornbusch, 1985, pp. 328–334), and the dollar area is growing faster than the world in general,[23] one may hypothesize that dollar commodity prices are becoming less sensitive to the dollar's exchange rate. Thus, the argument for Russia's anchoring the ruble to the dollar may be getting stronger.

The discussion of Central and Eastern Europe thus tends to two different conclusions. With the prospect of accession to the EU and the possibility of joining the monetary union in the next century, Eastern Europe might well enter naturally into the euro's orbit. Russia, with its Far East and commodity trade, and its current dollar orientation with regard to both exchange policy and private foreign-exchange holdings, is at least a closer call.

[21] The parameter estimate of the elasticity of commodity prices with respect to the dollar's effective exchange rate estimated at −0.62 by Borensztein and Reinhart (1994), does not contradict this statement. An effective dollar exchange rate is correlated with, but much less variable than, the dollar/mark rate. For evidence that the price of gold is more stable in dollars, see Murray, Klapwijk, le Roux, and Walker (1997, pp. 9–10).

[22] The greater-than-unit elasticity of the price of gold with respect to the dollar/mark exchange rate found by Dupont and Juan-Ramon (1996) may reflect the sample period, 1972–1991; see also Sjaastad and Scacciavillani (1996).

[23] The International Energy Agency (1996, pp. 26–27), projects that the "rest of the world"—that is, countries outside the Organisation for Economic Co-operation and Development (OECD) and the former Soviet bloc, which currently consumes about 30 percent of world oil—will account for 70 percent of the increase in world oil demand between 1993 and 2010. Evidence is presented below that the fastest-growing portion of this "rest of the world" remains in the dollar zone.

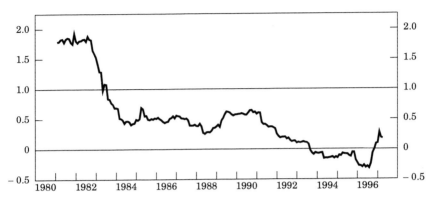

FIGURE 8

GOLD-PRICE SENSITIVITY TO MOVEMENTS IN THE MARK AGAINST THE DOLLAR
(*monthly averages*)

SOURCES: BIS and BIS calculations.

[a] Estimated, as in Figure 2, by regressing movements in the dollar price of gold on movements in the mark against the dollar over the current and previous thirty-six months.

Some Middle Eastern and North African currencies might also align themselves with the euro. As matters stand, Israel, Morocco, and Turkey seem to give substantial weight to European currencies in their currency management (Figure 7); the last two countries have expressed interest in joining the EU. The currencies of the oil-producing states, the Saudi Arabian riyal, for example, serve as a fire-break to the eastward spread of the euro, however. Farther south, the South African rand, much like gold, seems to have slipped from the deutsche mark zone into the dollar zone.

Whether the euro will disturb the dollar anchoring of currencies from South and East Asia to Latin America is an important question. Going beyond a quick look at the IMF's *Exchange Arrangements* (1997) compilation to conclude that "only a limited number of smaller countries" peg to the dollar (Krugman, 1984), several recent studies have investigated the behavior of Asian exchange rates. These exchange rates are anchored to the dollar, whether one performs multiple regressions (Frankel and Wei, 1993, 1994; Bénassy-Quéré, 1996a, 1996b), computes variance ratios (Bénassy-Quéré, 1996a, 1996b), or examines bilateral elasticities (BIS, 1997b). All the analysts agree that the yen, a more plausible anchor than the euro for some currencies in Asia, is hardly challenging the dollar as an anchor. As yet, Asian currencies show only limited co-movement with the yen (Figure 7).

Even before the recent currency turbulence in Asia, many economists recommended against the linkage of Asian currencies to the dollar and looked forward to the weaning of these currencies from it. Kwan (1994) concluded that patterns of international trade argue that the currencies of Hong Kong, Korea, Singapore, and Taiwan should be pegged to the yen. Eichengreen and Bayoumi (1996) suggested that the yen is a marginally better peg than the dollar for the currencies of Indonesia, Korea, and Thailand, and a not much worse peg for the currencies of several other countries. They suggested that "even Hong Kong, which has resisted greater flexibility to date, may have to contemplate it after the resumption of Chinese control in 1997," a notion that the Hong Kong authorities vigorously dispute.[24] This analysis, however, does not take into account the fact that other currencies, outside as well as inside Asia, are anchored to the dollar. Most Asian currencies have been almost completely surrounded by currencies anchored to the dollar. This circumstance is recognized by Williamson's (1996) proposal that Asian countries adopt a common currency basket for pegging, consisting of something like 40 percent in dollars, 30 percent in yen, and 30 percent in marks (then euro).[25] The analogy that Eichengreen and Bayoumi (1996) draw between Europe's movement away from the dollar in the 1970s and East Asia's situation today does not respect an important difference. From the outset of floating, a number of European currencies aligned themselves with the mark right away, so that a currency that moved into the mark's orbit later was joining an effective mark zone larger than Germany. In Asia, by contrast, the yen bloc has just one member.

Hamada (1994, p. 330) asks whether each Asian "country was driven by a purely economic rationale in its exchange-rate policy. In practice . . . political considerations may have motivated the pegging policy." This interpretation might suggest an increased willingness to anchor to the yen with the passage of time, much as Taiwan switched some of its dollar reserves into yen (Table 5). Taguchi (1994, p. 354), of the Bank of Japan, elaborates on the noneconomic considerations:

[24] Yam (1996) labeled the notion that Hong Kong will have to abandon its dollar peg "Myth Number Four."

[25] This sounds like the son of the Special Drawing Right (SDR), the IMF's hybrid basket currency. The introduction of the euro may provide the opportunity or excuse for a recasting of the SDR. At an IMF conference, Philippe Maystadt (1997) of Belgium raised the question whether the SDR should be based on only the dollar, euro, and yen. Governments propose but markets dispose, and markets have not embraced the SDR (Eichengreen and Frankel, 1996).

To what extent, and at what pace the Japanese yen will become an anchor currency in Asia hinges on many economic and noneconomic factors: e.g., how intraregional trade and investment will develop, the future military presence of the United States in this region, whether political ties among Asian countries become close and the development of the U.S. economy . . . [and, in particular, whether] the US economy remains sound and its inflation rate low.

If there is an argument for putting greater weight on the yen, is the argument getting stronger? Bénassy-Quéré (1996a, p. 19) notes that "there is a trade dynamism between non-Japan, Asian countries, . . . and the role of Japan as a trading partner is declining for most of the other Asian countries." As long as Asian currencies, apart from the yen, remained anchored to the dollar, this trade dynamism implied that the tide was running against the yen in Asia. Thus, even if the scant weight put on the yen in the management of Asian currencies was out of line with current trade relations, it was becoming less out of line with the passage of time. Another reason for anchoring to the dollar was its long downward trend against the yen. The dollar's rise against the yen from the spring of 1995 to the spring of 1997, however, rendered the dollar-linked Southeast Asian currencies uncompetitive.[26] The course of the dollar/yen rate will influence the choice of anchors in the years to come. Recent currency and banking instability in Southeast Asia raises the question of whether dollar anchoring is a thing of the past. When the dust settles, greater flexibility in exchange-rate systems is likely. The choice of a different anchor, however, is not a foregone conclusion.[27]

China presents a particularly interesting case in view of the growth of its economy and trade and the near-term prospect for its currency to become convertible and internationally tradable. Three-tenths of its exports go to the United States, as against about one-fifth to Japan and

[26] The observation that the Thais devalued the baht in 1984 (after a period of dollar appreciation) and adopted a basket peg thereafter, only to reduce sharply the weight of the yen in their basket in 1985 when the dollar started to fall against the yen, is consistent with this reading of the evidence. Another consideration, pointed out by Ueda (1994, p. 356) is that a stable consumer-price index in Japan implies a negative inflation rate for Japanese export prices, "creating strong deflationary pressure on other countries" linked to the yen. This argument is similar to that of Mundell (1993, p. 24), who maintains that "the deflationary stance of the [European] Community . . . will impose too tough a monetary standard for the countries of Eastern Europe to match. They are far more likely to adopt the easier standard that would be set by modest U.S. rates of inflation."

[27] See Ilzkovitz (1996) for a skeptical view of the prospects for the internationalization of the yen.

to the EU, whereas over one-fourth of its imports come from Japan, as against one-tenth from the United States and one-seventh from the EU. China's exports and the peg of the Hong Kong dollar to the U.S. dollar are cited by Hong Kong observers as reasons for the likely continuation of the anchoring of the Chinese currency to the dollar (Chen, 1997).

As for Latin America, its currencies are anchored to the dollar as strongly as ever. For some years, the Chilean peso was tied to a basket that assigned the dollar a weight of less than 50 percent, but as experience showed that dollar import prices did not fall as the dollar rose into 1997, the basket was revised to put a more typical weight on the dollar.

In summary, the euro does not face the chaos suggested by formal exchange-rate arrangements, which make floating exchange rates the overwhelming norm. Rather, the euro will come into existence surrounded by a "dollar zone, [which] far from breaking up since the collapse of the Bretton Woods system, . . . now encompasses the American continent[s], Asia, the Persian Gulf, Australia and New Zealand" (Ilzkovitz, 1995, p. 93). The policies of key countries now within the zone will determine the ambit of the euro.

The use of the euro as an anchor is related to its use in foreign-exchange-market transactions and its use as the currency of invoicing for international trade flows. Appendix D shows that, upon its introduction, the euro will be on one side of half or more foreign-exchange transactions, whereas the dollar will be on one side in almost all transactions. Appendix E considers trade invoicing, arguing that its importance is often misunderstood and overstated. The evidence, such as it is, suggests that the euro will start way behind the dollar as a unit of account for international trade, with little use by third parties outside the euro area. In particular, the notion that oil might be priced in euros seems to ignore the rapid growth of demand in dollar-linked emerging economies and the political developments in the 1990s.

Private Asset Managers

There is little disagreement that the introduction of the euro will create broader, deeper, and more liquid financial markets in Europe. Observers differ, however, on the prospects for an integrated government bond market in the euro area. A full discussion of these prospects can be found in McCauley and White (1997). The briefer review given here first highlights the size of the euro money market and swap market, demonstrating that these markets in euros will bulk large in comparison with their counterparts in dollars and yen. It then summarizes the evidence bearing on the prospects for an integrated government bond market in Europe.

Ranging from an overnight rate, which will be strongly affected by the monetary-policy operations of the ECB, to interbank rates for placements lasting from one week to one or two years, a single-reference money-market yield curve for euros can be expected. Its liquidity, as measured by derivatives transactions, will surpass that of the yen money market, even adopting the hypothesis of a narrow monetary union and recognizing the current influence of convergence trades (Table 7). A considerable gap will remain between the $40 trillion per year turnover in euro futures and forwards and the corresponding volume of dollar transactions, which exceed $100 trillion.

At longer maturities, the most frequently used private interest rates will be the yields on the fixed-rate side of interest-rate swaps. These standard and liquid prime-name rates extend from two years to ten years in maturity and already serve as the most important private reference rates in today's bond markets. The convergence among these swap yields for contracts in Belgian francs, German marks, Dutch guilders, and French francs over the past two years (Figure 9) underlies the forward rates displayed in Figure 2. At the introduction of the euro, the now nearly identical swap curves will collapse into a single swap curve.[28] This private capital market in euros is also likely to be a very liquid market from its inception. On current evidence, even a narrow monetary union would offer a swap market about as active as those in the dollar and yen (Table 8). Even recognizing again that convergence trades are providing a temporary boost to European transactions, the euro looks set to offer a private yield curve with world-class depth, breadth, and liquidity.

Those who argue that the government bond market in euros will be fractured point to the municipal bond market in the United States, where different states' bonds offer different yields as a result of widely differing credit standings and tax rates.[29] Current bond-market pricing and ratings, however, seem consistent with the development of nearly uniform valuations for certain European governments' bonds, which could then be interchangeably delivered into a futures contract (McCauley, 1996). At present, evidence points to very similar pricing of

[28] Illmanen (1997) considers why French franc forward swap rates have traded below their deutsche mark counterparts.

[29] The appropriateness of this analogy may be questioned in view of the strong clientele effects created by the state tax codes' exclusive tax exemption for interest on home-state municipal bonds.

TABLE 7

DERIVATIVES TRANSACTIONS IN PRIVATE MONEY-MARKET INSTRUMENTS
IN EUROS, DOLLARS, AND YEN
(*in trillions of dollars per annum*)

Currency	1995	1996
German mark		
Euro-mark futures (LIFFE)	17.960	24.090
Forward-rate agreements[a]	2.200	n.a.
Euro-mark options (LIFFE)	2.392	3.251
French franc		
PIBOR[b] contracts (MATIF)	15.513	13.818
Forward-rate agreements	2.593[c]	n.a.
PIBOR options (MATIF)	4.623	3.038
Italian lira		
Euro-lira futures (LIFFE)	2.459	4.497
Forward-rate agreements	0.451[c]	n.a.
Euro-lira options (LIFFE)	0.061	0.618
Total mark, franc, lira		
Euro-mark/franc/lira futures	35.932	42.405
Forward-rate agreements	5.244	n.a.
Euro-mark/franc/lira options	7.076	6.907
U.S. dollar		
Euro-dollar futures (CME, SIMEX)	104.125	97.068
Federal funds (CBOT)	3.219	3.042
Forward-rate agreements[a]	4.667	n.a.
Euro-dollar options (CME, SIMEX)	22.369	22.238
Japanese yen		
Euro-yen futures (TIFFE, SIMEX)	45.543	34.475
Forward-rate agreements[a]	2.518	n.a.
Euro-yen options (TIFFE, SIMEX)	0.521	0.714

SOURCES: London International Financial Futures and Options Exchange (LIFFE); Marché à Terme International de France (MATIF); Chicago Mercantile Exchange (CME); Singapore International Monetary Exchange (SIMEX); Chicago Board of Trade (CBOT); Tokyo International Financial Futures Exchange (TIFFE); BIS, *Central Bank Survey 1995*; BIS and author's estimates.

NOTE: Yen, mark, franc, and lira amounts are converted at year-average exchange rates.

[a] Estimated as average daily turnover in April *times* 255.

[b] Paris interbank offer rate.

[c] Estimated as mark forward-rate agreements (FRAs) *times* the ratio of FRA trading in Paris or Milan to FRA trading in Frankfurt.

FIGURE 9

PRIVATE INTEREST RATES IN EUROPE
(*in percent per annum*)

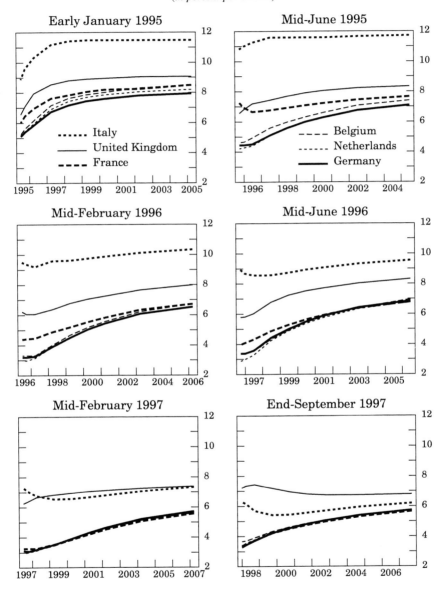

SOURCES: Datastream, Reuters, and BIS.

NOTE: The yield curves are based on eurodeposit rates and, for longer horizons, on swap (midpoint) yields.

TABLE 8

TRANSACTIONS IN INTEREST-RATE SWAPS AND SWAPTIONS IN EUROS,
DOLLARS, AND YEN
(in trillions of dollars per annum)

Currency	Central Bank Survey[a] 1995	International Swaps and Derivatives Association	
		1995	1996[b]
German mark	1.948	—	—
Swaps	1.661	0.985	1.935
Swaptions	0.287	—	—
French franc	2.303	—	—
Swaps	1.879[c]	1.113	1.550
Swaptions	0.424[d]	—	—
Italian lira	0.427	—	—
Swaps	0.367[c]	0.217	n.a.
Swaptions	0.060[d]	—	—
Total mark, franc, lira	4.678	—	—
Swaps	3.907	2.315	3.485
Swaptions	0.771	—	—
U.S. dollar	5.981	—	—
Swaps	4.283	2.856	3.690
Swaptions	1.698	—	—
Japanese yen	4.904	—	—
Swaps	4.378	2.259	3.128
Swaptions	0.527	—	—

SOURCES: ISDA; BIS, *Central Bank Survey 1995*; BIS and author's estimates.
[a] Estimated as average daily turnover in April *times* 255.
[b] First half, at annual rate.
[c] Estimated as mark swaps *times* the ratio of ISDA-reported French franc swaps or ISDA-reported Italian lira swaps to ISDA-reported mark swaps.
[d] Estimated as mark swaptions *times* the ratio of swaption transactions in Paris or Milan to such transactions in Frankfurt.

the creditworthiness of Dutch, French, and German government bonds. In particular, the gap between the nearly identical swap rates and the respective government-bond yields is practically the same in the three markets (Figure 10). Never in the history of the swap market has this spread been so similar for so long across so many markets.[30] This observation suggests that the euro-denominated debt of these

[30] The spread reflects not just the relative creditworthiness of the respective governments, but also cyclical factors, such as the strength of construction spending (Brown, 1989).

FIGURE 10

SPREADS OF TEN-YEAR GOVERNMENT YIELDS OVER INTEREST-RATE SWAP YIELDS
(*monthly averages, in basis points*)

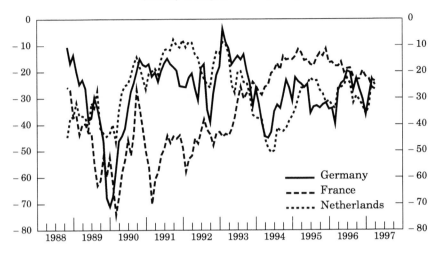

SOURCES: Datastream and Reuters.

governments will trade with nearly identical yields. Furthermore, major rating agencies assign the same top rating to the debts of Austria, France, Germany, and the Netherlands (see Table 1 and Cantor and Packer, 1996). Market participants want, and thoroughgoing integration would require, European treasuries to cooperate in establishing common market practices and conventions (European Commission, 1997a; Dammers, 1997). Joint auctions would not be necessary to build large benchmark issues; instead, European treasuries could simply match each other's terms, in effect "reopening" each other's issues. The potential benefit of integrated trading is evident in Table 9, which shows that the value of futures transactions in a European government bond market would compare favorably with that in Japan and would fall not far short of that in the United States.

The more integrated the government bond market in euros is, the more its liquidity and depth should improve. Both European residents and foreign investors could enjoy narrower bid-offer spreads, an ability to buy or sell larger amounts with no price effect, a richer array of instruments, and deeper repurchase markets. The euro bond market might be served by two active futures contracts, one at the medium term and the other at the long term, as the U.S. bond market now uniquely features (Jeanneau, 1995, 1996). Foreign investors might

37

TABLE 9

DERIVATIVES TRANSACTIONS IN LONG-TERM GOVERNMENT SECURITIES
IN EUROS, DOLLARS, AND YEN
(*in trillions of dollars per annum*)

Government bonds and notes	1995			1996		Memorandum	
	Futures	Exchange-Traded Options	Over-the-Counter Options[a]	Futures	Exchange-Traded Options	Cash Trading	Out-standings
German bonds	9.090	1.274	0.173	12.388	1.550	*16.566*	*0.727*
French bonds	3.367	0.954	0.256[b]	3.452	0.869	*1.658*	*0.490*
Italian bonds	1.610	0.156	0.036	2.008	0.340	*0.420[c]*	*0.391[d]*
Total German, French, and Italian bonds	14.067	2.384	0.465	17.848	2.759	*18.225*	*1.608*
U.S. Treasuries	12.374	3.627	0.435	12.011	3.667	*35.843*	*2.547*
Japanese bonds	15.956	2.163	1.539	12.262	1.824	*6.502*	*1.996*

SOURCES: Salomon Brothers; BIS, *Central Bank Survey 1995*; various futures exchanges; and national sources.

NOTE: Data on cash-market trading and outstandings are for 1995 and end-1995, respectively.

[a] Estimated as average daily turnover in April *times* 255.

[b] Estimated as OTC trading in interest-rate options on traded securities in marks *times* the ratio of total OTC trading in interest-rate options in Paris or Milan to that in Frankfurt.

[c] Euroclear and Cedel only.

[d] Lira-denominated treasury bonds only; excludes variable-rate notes.

come to enjoy trading opportunities in all major time zones, similar to those now available to holders of U.S. Treasuries.

In considering the potential for shifts by private portfolio managers into the euro, a difficult question arises as to whether interest rates in a large euro bond market might show a smaller correlation with U.S. bond yields than current European government bond rates display.[31] This is an interesting question, because private portfolio managers would find the euro bond market particularly attractive if it were to offer diversification benefits superior to anything available in the constituent bond markets. Large size and investor diversity could provide ballast to a European bond market now exposed to spillovers from New York (Borio and McCauley, 1996a, 1996b; Domanski and

---

[31] See also European Commission (1997b). Masson and Turtelboom (1997) simulate the change in the correlation of returns on short-term instruments only, deriving ambiguous results depending on the ECB's intermediate target. It is well known, however, that returns on short-term instruments are much less correlated than returns on bonds, so this interesting question remains wide open.

Neuhaus, 1996).[32] The trend toward higher correlations across European bond markets in recent years, however, has not brought any diminution of the correlation between the German and U.S. markets.

Greater liquidity and depth could increase the demand for bonds denominated in euros relative to the total demand for bonds in the constituent currencies, but the scope for a potential reallocation of private portfolios from the dollar to the euro is necessarily extremely conjectural. One starting point is provided by the shares across G–10 currencies of gross domestic product (GDP), trade, foreign-exchange reserves, and international assets, including both international bank deposits and international bonds (Figure 11). The G–10 members of the EU produce about one-third of G–10 output and would show a slightly smaller share of international trade net of their EU trade. After a similar consolidation, however, the share of international assets denominated in euros would be only about one-eighth of the G–10 total. For the euro share to match the output and trade shares of the G–10, members of the EU would require a shift of some $0.7 trillion. This figure should not be taken too seriously; the calculation ignores the nonresident holdings of one-quarter of U.S. Treasury securities and also the nonresident holdings of about one-third of German public bonds. The figure serves to make the important point, however, that shifts in private portfolios could prove to be much larger than any possible shifts in official reserves. Similar figures are produced on the backs of different envelopes by Bergsten (1997) and Thygesen et al. (1995).

Central Banks

Two hypotheses about diversification of official reserves away from the dollar by nonindustrial countries may provide an indicative range. If developing countries—admittedly a heterogeneous group, but the lack of available data constrains the discussion here—were to follow Taiwan's example in its diversification of the last ten years by increasing their portfolio weight on core Europe to 25 percent, about $85 billion could

---

[32] A contrary view is expressed by Thygesen et al. (1995, p. 126), who write:

Confidence in the insulating properties of flexible exchange rates was shattered from the first half of 1994 by the transmission of higher U.S. interest rates to Europe at a time when such a linkage seemed inappropriate because of different positions in the business cycle on the two sides of the Atlantic. At a time of high uncertainty in the foreign-exchange markets, investors appear to compare national interest rates more directly, discounting anticipated, but very uncertain, exchange-rate changes strongly in comparing the yield on assets denominated in different currencies. . . . A larger market share of the ECU [euro] in international financial portfolios and, hence, more symmetry between the dollar and the ECU [euro] would not really mitigate the problem.

FIGURE 11

THE INTERNATIONAL ROLES OF THE EURO, DOLLAR, AND YEN
(currency and country shares, in percentages)

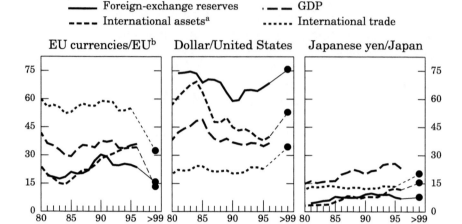

——— Foreign-exchange reserves   . — — GDP

- - - - International assets[a]   ...... International trade

SOURCES: IMF, OECD, BIS, and national data.

NOTE: Hypothetical shares beyond 1999 are computed by netting out from most recent observations: EU holdings of EU currency reserves, EU holdings of EU currency bank assets and EU issuers' bonds or notes in G–10 EU currencies, and G–10 EU trade with EU countries. Total reserves, assets, and G–10 GDP in 1996 were $1.52 trillion (1.38 consolidated total), $5.1 trillion (3.9 consolidated total), and $19.9 trillion, respectively; G–10 trade in 1995 was $5.8 trillion (3.9 consolidated total).

[a] Includes international bonds, cross-border bank liabilities to nonbanks, foreign-currency liabilities to domestic nonbanks (from 1984), and euronotes (from 1989).

[b] G–10 EU countries only.

be shifted out of the dollar and into the euro.[33] Were all nonindustrial countries to put equal weight on the euro and the dollar, some $200 billion could be shifted. This latter scenario, however, ignores the potential for reserve diversification by Asian central banks into the yen.

Even as such figures are contemplated, recall that official reserve status and currency strength are far from necessary companions. The

---

[33] As recently as end-1986, Taiwan's reserves were 95 percent dollars (Seth and McCauley, 1987, p. 37). Tavlas and Ozeki (1992, p. 40), however, report that even as Taiwan was diversifying away from the dollar, "selected [unnamed, unnumbered] Asian countries," presumably not including Taiwan, were raising their holdings of dollars from 48 percent in 1986 to 63 percent in 1990, at the expense of the yen and European currencies.

Swiss franc has tended to appreciate in real terms in recent years, and Switzerland has the dubious distinction of serving the most expensive McDonald's hamburgers in the world. Yet the fraction of the Swiss franc in official reserve portfolios has fallen from a peak near 3 percent in 1980 to 1 percent in 1996.

Global Liability Managers

Many analysts foresee that portfolio shifts by private investors and official reserve managers from the dollar into the euro will drive up the euro against the dollar and push the euro area from a current-account surplus into a current-account deficit (Bergsten, 1997; Alogoskoufis and Portes, 1997). This argument resembles that of Triffin (1960), who observed that the growth of world trade meant a growing demand for dollar-denominated bank accounts with which to settle the transactions.[34] If the only way for these dollars to reach the hands of traders outside the United States were for the latter to run deficits, Triffin argued, then the necessary succession of deficits would undermine the credibility of the link between the dollar and gold. Take away the problem of the gold link, and the line of reasoning put forward by Bergsten and by Alogoskoufis and Portes is very Triffinesque: a portfolio shift into the euro entails deficits for the euro area.

Kindleberger (1965) and Kindleberger, Despres, and Salant (1966) denied Triffin's claim that the United States had to run deficits in any reasonable sense of the word in order to provide the world with dollar balances. If the U.S. banking system were to extend long-term credits to foreign companies and governments, and the funds were to accumulate as short-term bank deposits, then the needs of trade could be met.[35] In application to the present case, the shift of private asset managers and official reserve managers into the euro need not push the euro upward in the exchange market or push the euro area into current-account deficit if willing borrowers of euros come forward.

This is likely because, in addition to having strong attractions for asset managers, a more integrated bond market in Europe would also attract debt managers in the steady state. (Debt management does not fit into

---

[34] I am indebted for this parallel to Paul De Grauwe, commenting at a Centre for Economic Policy Research seminar on exchange-rate policy for the euro.

[35] Although it is tempting to say that "Triffin had the better of the argument" (Garber, 1996, p. 2), it is fairer to say that "the cogency of that position [of Kindleberger, Despres, and Salant] has been thoroughly undermined by the fact that the United States has now developed a real [that is, a current-account] deficit" (Kindleberger, 1985, p. 295).

the above sections because the arguments apply to both official and private debt managers.) The development of a broad and deep euro bond market could potentially affect debt management more strongly than asset management, and the greater supply of euro-denominated assets could put downward pressure on the euro.

It may seem strange that something as welcome as the development of broad, deep, and liquid markets could adversely affect the currency concerned, but portfolio theory holds that the shift of funding from one currency to another will result in some combination of a higher interest rate and a lower exchange rate for the currency experiencing the increase in asset supply. For instance, were Korea to issue new deutsche mark securities and to use the proceeds to buy in all its dollar debt, private investors would need to be induced to hold more mark and fewer dollar assets. Depending on the size of the operation, some combination of higher deutsche mark interest rates and a lower mark exchange rate might be required to make the investors willing to hold newly supplied deutsche mark securities. A flow model of exchange-rate determination agrees with the result: as the Koreans exchanged the newly borrowed deutsche marks for the dollars required to pay off their outstanding dollar debts, the demand for dollars would rise. The current choice of currency for large issues by global debt managers and the current financing habitat of emerging economies make the prospect of heavier use of the euro by debt managers plausible.

The relation of the size of international bond issues to the choice of currency denomination suggests that more-liquid European bond markets might attract more borrowing. As matters stand, international bond issuers favor the dollar for large deals (Table 10). If an underwriter of a large bond issue in euros could more easily hedge against movements in the underlying euro yields by shorting large blocks of European government bonds, issuing costs might fall, eliminating this bias and inducing more issuance in euros. Although there is no guarantee that borrowers do not offset any constraint on their choice of currency for large debt issues by appropriately managing their other liabilities and assets, including those off balance sheet, the evidence suggests that market fragmentation in Europe might be keeping debt out of the euro's predecessor currencies.

With a broader, deeper, and more liquid bond market in Europe, moreover, debt managers outside Europe could be interested in increasing the proportion of their debt that is denominated in euros. The estimated currency composition of international debt (Table 11) owed by countries in Asia and Latin America shows a very low share of

TABLE 10

INTERNATIONAL SECURITY ISSUES BY SIZE AND CURRENCY

FROM 1990 TO 1995

(*in billions of U.S. dollars*)

Currency of Denomination	Less than $1 bn.	Greater or Equal to $1 bn.	Total
Developing countries	141.7	10.5	152.2
U.S. dollar	96.8	7.4	104.2
EU currencies	17.6	0.0	17.6
Japanese yen	27.3	3.2	30.5
Industrial countries	1,555.7	209.1	1,764.8
U.S. dollar	554.9	119.5	674.4
EU currencies	660.1	58.9	719.0
Japanese yen	340.8	30.6	371.4
International institutions	117.1	39.9	216.9
U.S. dollar	34.1	15.0	49.1
EU currencies	113.9	15.3	129.3
Japanese yen	29.1	9.5	38.6
Total	1,874.5	259.5	2,134.0
U.S. dollar	685.8	141.9	827.7
EU currencies	791.6	74.3	865.9
Japanese yen	397.1	43.3	440.4
Grand total, including offshore centers	2,078.6	276.9	2,355.5

SOURCES: Euromoney Bondware and BIS.
NOTE: Includes bonds and medium-term notes.

European currencies.[36] Even if the euro—or in Asia, the yen—does not displace the dollar as a reserve currency, there is great scope for additional borrowing in euros.[37] Currently, the weight of the European currencies in the reserves of nonindustrial countries (Table 5) is noticeably heavier than in the debt of those countries.

[36] Table 11 combines data collected by the World Bank and BIS. Compare Bénassy-Quéré (1996a, 1996b), who relies on World Bank data alone.

[37] Small EU countries such as Ireland and Portugal may be tempted to borrow exclusively in the broad and deep euro market, instead of using marks, dollars, and local and other currencies. For some EU countries, such a policy might miss an opportunity to use debt management as a substitute for exchange-rate flexibility. If a country has larger than EU-average trade shares with the dollar area, it is more exposed to a loss of exports resulting from a dollar depreciation. Whereas before, the tendency of the currency to fall against the mark served to buffer the economy against dollar depreciation, going forward, the economy could benefit from the interest savings on dollar-denominated debt in the event of dollar depreciation. Working in the opposite direction, it must be admitted,

43

TABLE 11

CURRENCY COMPOSITION OF DEVELOPING-COUNTRY DEBT AT END OF 1996

(in billions of U.S. dollars and percentages)

Obligor	U.S. Dollar	%	Japanese Yen	%	EU Currencies	%	Other[a]	%	Total	%
Latin America	421.1	(67.4)	66.0	(10.6)	72.0	(11.5)	65.2	(10.4)	624.3	(100.0)
To banks	100.3		2.2		7.1		4.2		113.7	
To World Bank[b]	320.8		63.8		65.0		61.0		510.7	
Asia	344.7	(46.3)	243.4	(32.7)	71.7	(9.6)	85.4	(11.5)	745.1	(100.0)
To banks	135.7		80.1		10.6		16.9		243.3	
To World Bank[c]	209.0		163.3		61.1		68.5		501.9	
Eastern Europe	138.0	(37.0)	42.6	(11.4)	101.9	(27.3)	90.9	(24.3)	373.4	(100.0)
To banks[d]	7.3		0.5		14.3		5.3		27.4	
To World Bank[e]	130.8		42.2		87.5		85.6		346.1	
Total[f]	1,044.5	(50.2)	377.1	(18.1)	329.4	(15.8)	331.4	(15.9)	2,082.5	(100.0)
To banks	245.0		73.9		32.9		22.3		374.1	
To World Bank	799.5		303.2		296.6		309.1		1,708.4	

SOURCES: World Bank and BIS.

NOTE: World Bank figures for 1996 are preliminary and refer to debt maturities greater than one year. Multiple-currency debt reported is distributed among underlying currencies according to the composition of the World Bank currency pool. Obligations to banks exclude bank claims of more than one-year maturity, including medium-term debt with remaining maturity of less than one year. Semiannual maturity distribution is applied to quarterly currency distribution. Includes author's estimates of currency breakdown of debt to banks in offshore centers and other debt to banks for which no official currency breakdown is available. Figures are rounded and may not sum to totals.

[a] Includes unidentified.
[b] Includes Caribbean.
[c] Includes East Asia, Pacific, and South Asia.
[d] Includes former Yugoslavia.
[e] Includes Europe and Central Asia.
[f] Includes Africa.

It is thus possible that a larger supply of euro-denominated assets, which on portfolio-balance reasoning would push down the value of the euro, could outweigh a larger demand, which would push it up.[38] At

---

is the new World Bank policy of offering its borrowers a choice in the denomination of credits. Previously, the World Bank mixed a currency cocktail, heavily weighted toward low-interest-rate currencies in Europe and the yen, and it gave its borrowers no choice but to accept the cocktail. Evidently, the World Bank will be lending a larger share of dollars under the new policy. I am indebted to Jeffrey Shafer for pointing out this "dollar-negative" factor to me.

[38] See Alogoskoufis, Portes, and Rey (1997) for the argument that the shift of assets into the euro should be expected to occur faster than the offsetting shift of liabilities. Their argument ignores the importance of short-term international debt and the capacity of currency swaps to transform exposures.

any rate, one should not attempt to calculate the effects of the greater attraction of the euro for official and private asset managers without considering that it might exert a similar attraction for debt managers.

Volatility

The question of the long-run effect of monetary union on the volatility of the dollar breaks into two issues: the volatility of the bilateral dollar/euro rate as compared with the historical volatility of the dollar/mark rate and the volatility of the effective dollar rate, that is, the average volatility of the dollar against the currencies of U.S. trading partners, each weighted by the importance of its trade.[39]

An often-heard view is that altered constraints on European monetary policy will leave the dollar more volatile against the euro than it has been against the mark. That is, many observers predict that, in the long run, the ECB will attach little importance to stabilizing the euro's exchange rate, pursuing, instead, a policy sometimes called "benign neglect." The argument starts with the observation that the euro area will be more closed than its constituent national economies, with a ratio of imports to domestic product in the neighborhood of one-tenth, as in the United States and Japan. Prices in the large euro area, potentially including currencies pegged to the euro, will therefore be less influenced by foreign prices as translated by the exchange rate. As a result, a given appreciation or depreciation of the euro will exert less deflationary or inflationary force, and the need to adjust interest rates to counter such force will be reduced accordingly (Kenen, 1995, pp. 122–123; Begg, Giavazzi, and Wyplosz, 1997, p. 15).[40]

This argument, in its bald form, ignores the considerable cohesion of European currencies in the face of dollar movements, which means that the single-currency result has already been approached to varying degrees. When that cohesion was severely strained in 1995, however, the dollar's depreciation passed through to an unusual extent into an effective appreciation of the mark, with unusually powerful effects on German exports and investment spending. Not just a weak dollar, but also weak European currencies against the mark, dampened activity in Germany and prompted interest-rate cuts.

---

[39] An intermediate question is how dollar/euro volatility might compare with dollar/ECU volatility. Thygesen et al. (1995, p. 129) suggest that volatility and cycles in the former will be larger than volatility and cycles in the latter, but their reasoning is not clear.

[40] See Martin (1997) for a treatment of this argument in the context of two countries with interacting policies.

The benign-neglect story might therefore be better phrased in the following fashion: Monetary union might reduce the policy salience of the exchange rate because dollar weakness will no longer be associated with European currency strains. Indeed, a weakening dollar has generally preceded realignments within Europe (Figure 3), most spectacularly, but by no means uniquely, in 1992, when the German economy needed the cooling-off of a strong mark, but the British and Italian economies did not.[41] With monetary union, European central bankers might spend fewer weekends worrying about the dollar's exchange rate.

Two policy counterarguments point in the opposite direction, however, suggesting that a dollar/euro exchange rate may be less volatile than the dollar/mark rate has been. The first is the implication of the wider domain of monetary policymaking in Europe after currency union (Dornbusch, Favero, and Giavazzi, 1997; Kenen, 1997). Interest-rate policy under the single currency will presumably respond, not to business conditions in one country, but rather to conditions in a large, possibly more heterogeneous, euro area. Whereas demand pressures in Germany might call for a sharp change in interest rates, conditions elsewhere might require no change at all. Recall the case of German reunification. Had the ECB been in existence, interest rates would not have climbed so high (quite apart from any national differences in tolerance of inflation). Given policy set with an eye to stabilizing activity in the euro area as a whole, the amplitude of European interest-rate swings from the trough to the peak of the European business cycle can be expected to be smaller.[42] In fact, before the 1990s, the output gap of the EU as a whole swung less widely than did the output gap for Germany, suggesting the potential for a more stable European interest-rate policy than the observed German policy (Figure 12).[43] Because the EU cycles and the U.S. cycles were no more out of synchronicity than were the German and U.S. cycles, there is reason to expect the dollar/euro rate to prove more stable than the dollar/mark rate.

[41] Figure 3 transforms the chart in Giavazzi and Giovannini (1989), recently updated by Buiter, Corsetti, and Pesenti (1997), into a "spider" diagram.

[42] See Masson and Turtelboom (1997) for a simulation with a very strong result in this direction. Artus (1996) argues that monetary policy will have to be more restrictive to respond to a given inflationary threat, however, because, given the size of the euro area, the effect of a stronger euro on domestic prices will be weaker than the effect of a stronger mark on German prices.

[43] For evidence of central-bank responses to the output gap, see Clarida, Gali, and Gertler (1997).

FIGURE 12

OUTPUT GAPS

(*in percentages*)

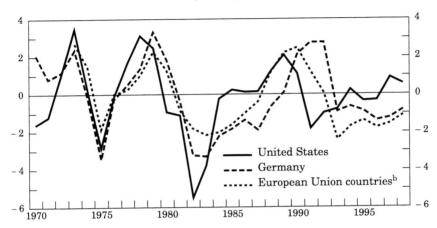

SOURCES: OECD, *Economic Outlook*, June 1997; EMI, *Annual Report 1994*.
NOTE: Shows deviations of actual GDP from potential GDP as a percentage of the latter.
[a] Weighted by central banks' shares of EMI's financial resources.

Another policy argument posits a difference in policy preferences reflected in the membership of the ECB's board. If national preferences for effective exchange-rate stability differ, the collective determination of European monetary policy in the ECB could increase the policy weight placed on exchange-rate stability. Although the core European countries as a group have shown quite stable effective exchange rates, the deutsche mark has displayed somewhat higher volatility than its neighboring currencies (Table 12). If this record manifests policy preferences, rather than mere size differences, the euro's managers might be expected to try harder to stabilize the euro, and might even succeed.

Without taking a view on the balance of these conflicting opinions about the way in which dollar/euro volatility will compare to dollar/mark volatility, it is still possible to come to a presumption regarding the volatility of the effective dollar rate, which represents at the same time a presumption regarding the volatility of the effective euro. The effective dollar rate has tended to be much less volatile than either the dollar/mark or the dollar/yen rate. This relative stability has resulted from the comparatively low volatility of currencies in the large area over which the dollar is used as an anchor, including parts of Asia, but it also derives from the less-than-perfect correlation of European exchange rates against the dollar (Figure 2). It follows that monetary

47

TABLE 12

VOLATILITY OF NOMINAL EFFECTIVE EXCHANGE RATES

(*annual averages, in percentages*)

Country	1983[a]–96	1993–94	1995–96
Belgium	2.5	3.0	2.6
Netherlands	2.8	2.6	3.0
France	2.9	2.8	3.0
Denmark	3.0	3.2	2.7
Spain	3.3	4.6	3.1
Germany	3.4	3.7	3.9
Canada	3.5	4.4	4.1
Italy	3.7	5.4	6.3
Sweden	3.9	6.8	5.6
United States	4.7	4.2	3.8
United Kingdom	5.2	4.9	4.3
Japan	6.4	7.2	7.4
Australia	7.5	8.0	7.1

SOURCE: BIS.

NOTE: Volatility is measured as the annualized standard deviation of daily percentage changes in nominal effective exchange rates calculated over a calendar month. Nominal effective exchange rates are based on trade flows in manufactured goods among twenty-five countries.

[a] October through December.

union in Europe, which will effectively raise the correlations of a group of dollar exchange rates to unity, will render the effective dollar rate more volatile, other things being equal.[44] If the dollar/euro exchange rate is no less volatile than the dollar/mark exchange rate has been, it is fairly likely that the effective dollar rate will be more volatile with a single currency in Europe. This statement is close to a tautology, but it gains some support from observations of the dollar's effective volatility over the last generation.

Going beyond theoretical analyses of the prospective volatility of the euro (Bénassy-Quéré, Mojon, and Pisani-Ferry, 1997; Cohen, 1997), consider the "natural experiment" represented by observations of the volatility of the effective dollar rate in periods defined by the different degrees of cohesion among European currencies. The effective dollar rate has generally been more volatile since European currencies moved

---

[44] Thus, a conclusion that the EMS had no effect on the dollar's volatility cannot be drawn by examining the volatility of the bilateral exchange rates between the dollar and each European currency without regard to the covariances; see Edison and Kole (1994).

into the deutsche mark's orbit in the late 1970s.[45] The effective dollar's volatility averaged about 9 percent during the narrow-band period from 1979 to 1992 and reached even higher levels during the "hard" ERM period from 1987 to 1992. Since September 1992, this volatility has tended to fall, and it has averaged about 7 percent since the widening of the ERM bands in the summer of 1993 (Figure 13). In short, the volatility of the effective dollar rate was highest when European rates were most cohesive, is middling now with generally wide bands, and was lowest before the ERM.[46] Looking forward, monetary union is likely to take the dollar's effective volatility back up to the levels of the 1980s.[47]

Summary

There is no immediate prospect for the euro's use as an anchor currency outside Central Europe and the Mediterranean. Still, a successful euro could deepen Europe's financial markets and conceivably make the evolution of European bond prices more independent of developments in New York. Both greater depth and better diversification possibilities could attract more international investment to the euro. The prospect of substantial portfolio shifts into the euro, however, does not by itself justify forecasts that the new currency will appreciate against the dollar over an extended period. Liability managers outside the euro area should also find attractive the enhanced liquidity and improved diversification possibilities of euro-denominated debt. Thus, in response to a shift in demand, global financial markets are capable of producing euro-denominated assets through changes in the currency habitats of international borrowers. Even if there are net (*ex ante*) shifts into the euro, their impact on the exchange rate could be smaller than is generally believed (see Appendix A).

---

[45] Padoa-Schioppa (1985), demonstrating that the EMS had succeeded in mapping out a zone of monetary stability, showed that European currencies experienced lower volatility in the period from March 1979 to March 1984 than they had in the period from March 1973 to March 1979, whereas the dollar, pound, and yen all experienced higher volatility. Padoa-Schioppa did not entertain the possibility that the cohesion of the European currencies might be connected to the higher volatility of the other currencies.

[46] These observations need not contradict the cross-sectional result of Martin (1997, p. 8), who finds that "EMS currencies have a lower volatility with currencies not in the EMS."

[47] In all likelihood, the larger the euro area, the higher the dollar volatility; see Ghironi and Giavazzi (1997) for implications of the size of the euro area.

FIGURE 13

EFFECTIVE DOLLAR VOLATILITY AND EUROPEAN CURRENCY COHESION
(*in percentages*)

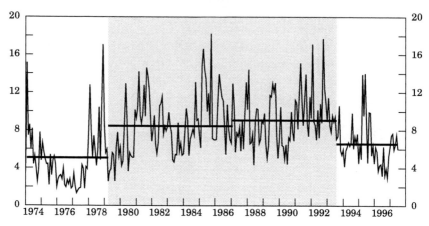

NOTE: Volatility is measured as the annualized standard deviation of daily percentage changes during calendar months in the Federal Reserve index for the effective exchange rate of the dollar. The weight of the European currencies in that index is 77.3 percent. The horizontal lines indicate the average volatility for the periods January 1974 through February 1979, March 1979 through December 1986, January 1987 through July 1993 (excluding September 1992), and August 1993 through June 1997. The shaded area represents the period during which narrow ERM bands prevailed (March 1979 through July 1993).

With respect to volatility, there are grounds for expecting a more volatile effective exchange rate for the dollar. In the absence of the buffering effect of the systematic tendency of European exchange rates to weaken against the mark when the dollar does so, the dollar is likely to move more widely against the weighted average of U.S. trading-partner currencies.

5 Conclusions

Broad monetary union in Europe would introduce a euro that would generally carry more weight as an international money than the mark carries but less weight than currently adheres to the sum of the euro's constituent currencies. In the foreign-exchange market, the euro is likely to be on one side of 50 to 60 percent of all transactions, more than the mark's 37 percent but less than the 70 percent share of all EU currencies at present. In the invoicing of international trade, the euro is likely to denominate something like one-quarter of world trade, more than the mark's one-sixth, but less than the combined EU currencies' one-third. As a reserve currency, the euro is likely to claim a share of about one-sixth, much the same as the mark, and lower than the one-fifth claimed by all EU currencies (including the pound). In terms of international private assets, the euro's likely share of one-seventh would be no higher than the mark's current share and would be half of the EU currencies' joint share. When one compares the euro's prospective role to the one-third share of the EU G–10 countries in G–10 GDP or international trade, one can readily conclude that the euro's economic base would support a larger role of the euro as an international money. Add to these comparisons an increase in the breadth, depth, and liquidity of the European financial markets, with the possible implication of greater independence of returns in European fixed-income markets from those in New York, and the potential for the euro as an international money comes into view.

But the very act of monetary union will tend to push up the dollar's share on all these measures (Table 13). In the foreign-exchange market, 92 percent of transactions would have the dollar on one side. In trade invoicing, the dollar would serve as the currency of contract for 59 percent of all transactions. As a reserve currency, the dollar would represent three-quarters of all holdings. And among international private assets, the dollar's share would rise to 50 percent. From one perspective, the rise of the dollar on these measures is uninteresting, reflecting as it does the merely arithmetic effect of treating the EU as a single monetary area.[48] After all, although intra-European foreign-exchange transactions will indeed disappear—to the considerable benefit of Europeans (Emerson et al., 1992)—a Martian would discern no visible change in economic activity: European trade would continue and might grow faster; European central banks would have domestic assets instead of foreign assets; and European borrowers would continue to sell their bonds to Europeans in other countries (perhaps more so), even if no longer denominated in a foreign currency. From another perspective, however, the rise of the dollar's share on these measures points to the limited, regional, success of the mark as a vehicle currency in foreign-exchange transactions, as an official reserve currency and as

[48] But see Eichengreen and Frankel (1996, p. 371), who suggest that "if a larger share of world reserves is denominated in dollars, network-externality effects may encourage countries to accumulate even more." Padoa-Schioppa and Saccomanni (1996, p. 380) play down such transactions costs and conclude that "the demand for dollars as a reserve currency might indeed be subject to major reversals should policy conflicts emerge and persist."

TABLE 13

INTERNATIONAL USES OF MAJOR CURRENCIES BEFORE AND AFTER
THE EURO

(*in percentages*)

Use	Currency	Before	After
Official reserves[a]	EU currencies/euro	24	16
	Dollar	69	76
	Yen	7	8
International assets	EU currencies/euro	34	13
	Dollar	40	53
	Yen	12	15
Foreign-exchange	EU currencies/euro	70	56
transactions[b]	Dollar	84	92
	Yen	24	26
Denomination of	EU currencies/euro	34	22
trade	Dollar	48	59
	Yen	5	6
Memorandum:			
GDP as % of G-10	*Euro-Area G-10*	*36*	*36*
	United States	*37*	*37*
	Japan	*23*	*23*
International trade	*Euro-Area G-10*	*55*	*32*
as % of G-10	*United States*	*23*	*34*
	Japan	*13*	*20*

SOURCES: BIS, *Central Bank Survey 1995*; Consensus Economics, *Consensus Forecasts*, August 1996; Hartmann, "The Future of the Euro," 1996, p. 7 (citing Ilzkovitz, 1995); United Nations (for trade data); IMF; BIS and author's estimates.

[a] Shares are rounded and sum to 100, despite the Swiss franc's 1 percent share.

[b] Figures represent the turnover in which a given currency appears on one side of a transaction; consequently, the percentages sum to 200 (including currencies not shown).

a standard of deferred payment. In a world of unbalanced growth, this regional focus of the mark as an international money has consequences for the prospective role of the euro.

The rapid growth of output and international trade in Asia, its spread to the larger economies of the region, and the general dollar orientation of Asian exchange-rate policies imply that the dollar area has been growing faster that the world economy as a whole. (If the U.S. economy continues to grow faster than the rest of the G–10 economies, the pattern of growth across the G–10 countries will only reinforce the broader trend.) To be sure, the introduction of the euro will effectively enlarge the European currency zone by eliminating the gravitational effects of the dollar on the economies at the edges of Europe (Figure 2). But this enlargement, which may occur in several stages and eventually include the countries of central Europe, is contrary to the general movement in the opposite direction produced by faster growth in economies more oriented toward the dollar. Dollar Telephone and Telegraph is installing many new lines in young countries, but Euro Telephone and Telegraph will not, on current trends, enjoy such customer growth after it has finished rewiring central Europe.

Some analysts have therefore discerned signs of a leveling off or even reversal in the 1990s of the long decline in the dollar's role (Oppers, 1995; Frankel, 1995; Eichengreen and Frankel, 1996), a role that in any case was subject to overstatement (Kenen, 1983). Changing the metaphor, the plate tectonics of the global economy, by adding to the economic mass of parts of the world where wealth is still measured in dollars, may serve to sustain and even to increase the dollar's role.

Looking further ahead, there is no guarantee that the dollar area will continue to grow more rapidly than the world as a whole on the basis of rapidly growing Asian economies linked to the dollar. By mid-1997, growth prospects had darkened for some Asian countries. The depreciation of Asian exchange rates in the summer of 1997, moreover, put their dollar anchoring in question and may give rise to a larger role for the yen and the euro.

What needs to be borne in mind, though, is the ambiguity of the relation between the respective international roles of the euro and the dollar, on the one hand, and the exchange rate between them, on the other. Were the euro to figure more importantly in the management of industrializing economies currently tied to the dollar, asset managers *and* liability managers there would be more likely to shift their portfolios toward the euro. Because these countries are generally running current-account deficits and thereby accumulating international debt, however, such a portfolio shift from the dollar to the euro would tend to produce a lower exchange rate for the euro against the dollar.

Thus, however the euro, dollar, and yen stand in relation to each other as international moneys a generation from now, the best prediction is that the exchange rate of the euro will reflect inflation outcomes, growth performance, and long-term developments in net-foreign-asset positions on both sides of the Atlantic. Over shorter horizons, the relation between business cycles and associated cycles in monetary policy will figure importantly in variations in the dollar/euro rate. Portfolio flows between the euro and the dollar might at times exert a powerful force, but they are unlikely to run so much in one direction that they predominate in setting the dollar/euro rate.

Appendix A: Quantitative Effects of Portfolio Shifts

This appendix tackles two different aspects of portfolio shifts from the dollar into the euro. First, it considers the implications of shifts from dollar cash into euro cash holdings by residents of third countries. Second, given *ex ante* shifts from the dollar by official or private asset managers, it asks what order of magnitude of change can be expected in exchange rates.

Effects of Redistributing Seigniorage

When considering the effect of monetary union on the international role of the dollar, it is important to keep in mind what is *not* at stake. One such matter is a large flow of seigniorage, the interest savings to the U.S. Treasury that result from the holding by foreigners of hundred-dollar bills. Official reserves bear interest and so do not convey a windfall to the issuing country. (Although U.S. Treasury bills may yield slightly less owing to the substantial share held by foreign central banks, the roughly 10 percent higher yields paid on private instruments such as bank deposits mostly reflect liquidity and default-risk differences.) Countries can and do borrow to build up their reserves, so reserve accumulation need not entail a resource transfer to the reserve-currency country. The intermediation margin between dollar borrowing rates and returns on dollar reserve holdings is determined in competitive markets, and large bank deposits in the United States no longer attract a reserve requirement. This margin, moreover, need not accrue to the nationals of the reserve-currency country; indeed, a substantial fraction of official dollar reserves, perhaps one-quarter, appears to be held outside the United States (BIS, 1997b, p. 83). Furthermore, foreign branches and agencies in the United States receive some fraction of official dollar deposits. Similarly, the private use of the dollar typically does not convey seigniorage to the United States.[49]

Only holdings of dollar cash by foreigners (estimated at more than $200 billion) pay an annual tribute (estimated at $12 billion) in the form

---

[49] For an opposing view, see Tavlas (1991, p. 12).

of interest savings (Porter and Judson, 1996; Johnson, 1994). Even those analysts of European monetary union who foresee a significant shift of this seigniorage toward the euro have estimated a stream of seigniorage measured in single-digit billion-dollar figures and have recognized its tiny potential contribution to Europe's GDP.[50] Indeed, when the substitution of euro notes for mark notes occurs in the new millennium, there is a risk that the stock of mark notes held outside Germany might not be replaced by crisp new euro notes but might instead be put into interest-bearing bank accounts or even dollar cash. At risk here is a current flow of seigniorage to Germany (at 3 percent per annum) of DM 2 to 3 billion. Note that, despite counterfeiting problems, the U.S. Treasury was careful not to force the exchange of old hundred-dollar bills for newly introduced bills, lest the new Ben Franklin notes not return to sterile mattresses, stashes, and safe-deposit boxes.

Effects of Portfolio Shifts

As for the exchange-rate effect of the portfolio shifts described above, a quantitative perspective is useful (see Hung, Pigott, and Rodrigues, 1989). The stock of debt issued by the governments of the G–10 countries is about $10 trillion. In a somewhat stylized case of $3 trillion of debt in dollars and an equivalent amount in euros, a $30 billion supply shift from dollars into euros represents about 1 percent of either debt stock. If interest rates do not respond, so that the half-and-half portfolio demands are not disturbed, the dollar would have to fall by 2 percent against the euro to restore portfolio balance. Such an exchange-rate change is not much more than the standard deviation of one week's movement in the dollar/mark rate. In this example, moreover, the underlying asset stock and the exclusion of interest-rate effects both work to increase the hypothetical exchange-rate effect of the $30 billion shift.

---

[50] See Alogoskoufis and Portes (1991, p. 241). Emerson et al. (1992), using an estimate of $100 billion for offshore dollar cash, "guesstimate" that one-third of that amount could shift into ECUs, which at a 7 percent nominal interest rate, would generate $2.5 billion of seigniorage per year, or 0.045 percent of EU GDP. If one doubles the $100 billion, halves the interest rate, and makes some allowance for the DM 65 to 90 billion estimated by the Bundesbank (1995, p. 70) to be already circulating in Turkey, Poland, and elsewhere, the seigniorage would remain a single-digit billion-dollar equivalent, making a 0.0-something contribution to EU GDP. Alogoskoufis and Portes (1992, p. 292) produce an estimate similar to that of Emerson et al. Johnson (1996, p. 165) considers the case in which $100 billion in euro notes are held outside the euro area. See Rogoff (1997) for a discussion of the merits and demerits of international competition for seigniorage.

Under more realistic assumptions, the long-run effect of even triple-digit portfolio shifts would not stand out in monthly trading, although some short-run digestion of shifts might be noticeable for a time.

Appendix B: Dollar/Mark Polarization and the Swiss Franc

In February 1996, the head of the Swiss Federal Department for Economic Affairs asked a commission comprising academics and bureaucrats, with representation of employers, employees, and bankers, to report on the implications of European monetary union for the Swiss economy. The commission's (Commission, 1996) view that capital is already fleeing the euro area into Switzerland has already been noted above, as has the Bundesbank's view that no solid evidence exists for this conclusion. The available data give little hint as to the origins of funds in trust accounts of Swiss banks, although there are suggestive observations, such as the *Wall Street Journal* headline earlier this year, stating "More German Banks Are Opening Swiss Units" (Wiesman, 1997). In any case, the Swiss commission's report concluded famously with some contingency planning: if the flight of capital into Switzerland threatened to push the franc to unbearable heights, the franc could temporarily be pegged to the euro.[51] Swiss National Bank authorities have from time to time repeated this possibility publicly, which is perhaps the monetary equivalent of letting potential invaders know that dynamite is already set in your tunnels and under your bridges.

A potentially important implication for the Swiss franc, which was apparently not considered by the commission,[52] arises from the historical pattern of exchange-rate changes in conjunction with the scale of the core European holdings of deutsche mark deposits. A long-observed regularity in exchange markets is that deutsche mark strength against the dollar is often associated with weakness of most European currencies against the mark (Figure 2). This dollar-mark polarization has presented a useful risk-reduction possibility for European investors. For a French investor, for instance, holding deutsche mark assets has offered a useful hedge against dollar assets: when the dollar has declined against the French franc, the mark has tended to rise. Partly for this reason, nonbank residents of France, Belgium, the Netherlands,

---

[51] An interesting question is whether Swiss interest rates would rise or fall under these circumstances (see Mauro, 1996).

[52] Or by Laxton and Prasad (1997), although they may have modeled it as a persistent portfolio-preference shift.

and Austria hold mark deposits in London, Frankfurt, and elsewhere (Table B–1). Were European exchange rates to be fixed, this negative covariance would disappear. The Swiss franc would most likely remain as an alternative, however, and it might become more attractive in international portfolios as a result of its greater scarcity.[53] The Swiss franc tends to appreciate against the deutsche mark when the mark appreciates against the dollar. Given this tendency, the worst scenarios in terms of the potential appreciation of the Swiss franc would be ones in which the deutsche mark rises, for instance, a noncredible delay in the start of monetary union.

If this nexus among dollars, marks, and Swiss francs is expected to reproduce itself, after the start of monetary union, as a nexus among dollars, euros, and Swiss francs, some potential responses by private investors merit consideration. Some of the $98 billion equivalent of deutsche mark bank accounts held by the residents of core European countries might be reinvested in the Swiss franc. To date, most of the

TABLE B–1

HOLDINGS OF MARK, SWISS FRANC, AND DOLLAR BANK DEPOSITS
BY RESIDENTS OF CORE EU COUNTRIES
AT END OF 1996
(*in billions of U.S. dollars*)

Country	German Marks	Swiss Francs	U.S. Dollars	Total
Germany	—[a]	3.5	17.7	21.2
France	9.3	3.5	24.8	37.6
Netherlands	53.4	5.1	30.6	89.1
Belgium/Luxembourg	23.5	4.2	32.5	60.2
Austria	11.8	0.6	3.6	16.0
Total Core EU	98.0	16.9	109.2	224.1

SOURCE: BIS.
NOTE: Nonbank holdings only.
[a] Deutsche mark deposits made by German residents in non-German banks amount to $149.8 billion.

[53] Eichengreen (1992, p. 58), suggests that "following EMU, investors in countries like France will have most of their wealth denominated in units of the single European currency. To minimize the risks caused by its fluctuation, they may find it attractive to hold additional dollars." But the Swiss franc might substitute for the lost services of the deutsche mark better than would the dollar.

reports of EMU-related investment in the Swiss franc have centered on German residents redeploying their wealth. Given the disappearance of a negative covariance in dollar and deutsche mark returns for French, Belgian, Dutch, and Austrian assets, some reallocation of their portfolios might be expected.

In the long run, the development of euro financial markets (McCauley and White, 1997) may reduce the sensitivity of the Swiss franc/euro exchange rate to movements in the dollar/euro exchange rate (as compared with the sensitivity of the Swiss franc/mark rate to the dollar/mark rate). Following the argument of Galati and McCauley (1997) that the Swiss franc owes its extreme position in the dollar/mark axis to the disproportionate importance of international investment in the Swiss franc, the internationalization of the euro in comparison with its constituent currencies should lead to better balance between the Swiss franc and the euro, and, thus, to less volatility in their exchange rate. This seems to be the conclusion, and the grounds for reaching it, of the Swiss commission (Commission, 1996, p. 3):

> The more stable the Euro becomes and the more liquid monetary and financial markets in the EMU are, the more the Euro should establish itself as a currency for international investment, thereby competing against the Swiss franc. The risk of an increased volatility of the exchange rate of the Swiss franc resulting from the substantial difference in size between the European monetary zone and Switzerland will decrease.

Appendix C: Resources, Constraints, and Incentives of European Official Reserve Managers

This appendix considers reserve management by European central banks in the transition stage and in the steady state and makes plausible estimates of the current composition of EU reserves. It must be said, however, that foreign-exchange reserves reflect past intervention and that they can rise or fall unpredictably even over a year or two. In particular, they can change markedly in any period of exchange-market turbulence. That said, should one expect European central banks to sell marks in the approach to monetary union but to sell dollars in its aftermath?

Switches into Dollars in the Transition Stage?

In the transition stage, purchases of dollars in the market could occur if participating central banks wished to preserve as foreign-exchange

TABLE C–1

THE COMPOSITION OF EU FOREIGN-EXCHANGE RESERVES AT END OF 1996

(*in billions of U.S. dollars and percentages*)

Currency	Core EU[a]	%	Core EU w/o Germany	%	Other EU[b]	%	Total	%
Core EU	33	(23)	33	(45)	92	(45)	126	(36)
Other	109	(77)	40	(55)	113	(55)	222	(64)
Total	142	(100)	74	(100)	206	(100)	348	(100)

SOURCES: IMF; BIS and author's estimates.

NOTE: Foreign-exchange reserves are calculated as total foreign-exchange reserves reported by the IMF *less* one-fifth of gold reserves (at end-September), assumed to have been swapped for ECUs. It is assumed that 45 percent of the reserves of both the core (excluding Germany) and other EU countries are held in core European currencies. "Other" currency is mostly dollars. Components are rounded and may not sum to totals.

[a] Austria, Belgium, France, Germany, Luxembourg, and the Netherlands (and ECUs with respect to currencies).

[b] Denmark, Finland, Greece, Ireland, Italy, Portugal, Spain, Sweden, and the United Kingdom.

reserves their substantial holdings of deutsche marks and other core European currencies. The scale of these holdings, estimated at $126 billion, or a little more than one-third of total EU foreign-exchange reserves of $348 billion at the end of 1996, makes this an interesting possibility (see Table C–1).[54] If dollar weakness does not give those central banks an opportunity to intervene and sell marks against dollars, and off-market transactions are not possible, some portion of the estimated $126 billion can be sold on the market this year or next. The possible motives for such conversions are by no means obvious. The rules for sharing the seigniorage arising from non-interest-bearing euro

---

[54] Compare Kenen (1995, p. 114), who reports that EU countries held "more than a quarter" of their foreign-exchange reserves in EU currencies in September 1991, according to calculations based on unpublished IMF data, and who writes (1996, p. 24) that "the deutsche mark holdings of EU countries probably account for about 20 percent of EU foreign-exchange reserves and for about 25 percent of the currency reserves of EU countries other than Germany." Also see Gros and Thygesen (1992), who put EU foreign-currency reserves held in EU currencies at 40 percent (p. 403) or at 55 percent (p. 254), and Masson and Turtelboom (1997, p. 205), who appear to treat all ECUs as official ECUs.

liabilities of the European System of Central Banks (ESCB) could conceivably provide an incentive to hold dollars from the start of the ECB.[55] But the incentive might pertain less to income or wealth than to power: the rules of the ECB could leave the national central banks more discretion over their (residual) foreign-currency assets than over their domestic assets. Sheer uncertainty with respect to either the economic or political implications of a central bank's asset composition might also recommend a switch into dollars.

Several considerations, however, render the prospect of large and possibly disruptive switches into dollars less likely in the near term: the possibility that some European currencies will remain outside the currency union for a time; the attractions of a passive strategy; and the fact that the first round of reserve pooling is unlikely to force sales of marks for dollars. If some EU countries were not to join monetary union initially, they might well need holdings of marks (and then euros) and might even seek to hold more reserves in core European currencies (or in euros) to back their commitments under an ERM II. This would hold especially if these "outs" (or so-called "pre-ins") were to anticipate that the market for exchanges of their domestic currencies against the euro would gain relative to the market for exchanges against the dollar.[56]

For central banks entering the monetary union, the alternative of inaction would permit reserves currently held in European currencies to be transformed into euros and invested in domestic assets. Central banks that anticipate an excess of foreign-exchange reserves under the single currency (see below) might find this do-nothing strategy attractive. It has been suggested that this course would be compelling because, as the reserves become euros, they could be used to retire

---

[55] The intention is to distribute the euro's seigniorage according to the shares shown in Table C–2. The problem then becomes how to identify the seigniorage. The European Monetary Institute (1997, p. 77) reports that the method for identifying seigniorage foreseen in Article 32.2 of the ESCB/ECB Statute was to earmark assets corresponding to cash and bank reserves and to pool the actual income earned on those assets. Difficulties in harmonizing central-bank accounting, however, have led to work on an alternative method, which could be used for up to five years. Under this alternative method, income would be imputed to the assets corresponding to cash and bank-reserve liabilities, using the monthly repo rate on euros (see "Dispute," 1997, p. 8). At a time of record low European short-term rates, a central bank concerned about its income—and skeptical about the Fisher open-interest-parity hypothesis—might prefer dollar to euro assets.

[56] This would reverse the gain in dollar transactions relative to mark transactions shown in exchanges against the lira and British pound between 1992 and 1995 (BIS, 1996b, p. 96). For the link between the currency composition of transactions and the composition of reserves, see Dooley, Lizondo, and Mathieson (1989).

government debt (Persaud and Dambassinas, 1996). Strictly speaking, however, any transfer of euros from a central bank to its treasury would have to take the form of a special dividend paid out of the central bank's retained earnings.[57] As suggested by the dispute over the German government's proposal to take into its budget some of the unrealized gains on the Bundesbank's gold holdings, such a special dividend raises questions among some European central banks. After all, the Maastricht Treaty prohibits central-bank financing of governments. Gros and Thygesen make the point that investing the central bank's former marks, now euros, in domestic government debt is economically equivalent to handing the proceeds over to the government for debt reduction.[58] Indeed, the economic effect of shifting former marks (now euros) out of German government debt and into domestic government debt would be visible only as a small change in the spread between the yield on German government debt and domestic government debt.

It is important to recognize that the first round of reserve pooling by the European central banks is unlikely to force sales of marks against dollars. In principle, an EU member having a high proportion of marks in its foreign-exchange reserves could be forced to buy dollars because "only assets denominated in currencies of non-EU Member States and gold will be eligible for transfer to the ECB" (EMI, 1995, p. 57). But the numbers suggest that forced sales of marks against dollars are unlikely. Three scenarios for the initial pooling merit consideration (Table C–2).[59] In the first, European central banks contribute *only* foreign exchange to the agreed upon initial ECU 50 billion pooling. In the second and third scenarios, gold as well as foreign exchange is pooled. (These latter scenarios have some of the flavor of the transactions underlying the creation of official ECUs, for which central banks swap a given fraction of their dollar and gold holdings.) In no case does the pooling demand a fraction of non-European reserves that is large enough to force sales of marks for dollars. Of course, further amounts can be pooled after appropriate agreement.

[57] Such a payment could also be made out of any gains recorded when mark-denominated reserves become euros (if, for instance, marks were carried at historical values in terms of domestic currency on the central bank's balance sheet) or from a revaluation of gold holdings.

[58] Gros and Thygesen (1992, p. 254) suggest that "from an economic point of view it does not matter how these former foreign exchange reserves are used. The net worth of the government (aggregating central bank and treasury) does not change when, for example, foreign exchange reserves are used to retire public debt."

[59] Compare Gros and Thygesen (1992, p. 403), who set out country-by-country reserve holdings of non-EU currencies and compare them with pooling needs.

TABLE C–2

RESERVE POOLING OF ECU 50 BILLION AT THE EUROPEAN CENTRAL BANK AT END OF 1996:
THREE SCENARIOS
(in billions of U.S. dollars and percentages)

Country	Weight (%)	FX Re-serves[a]	Gold Re-serves[b]	Only FX Pooled		Equal Amounts of FX & Gold Pooled			Equal Propor-tions of FX & Gold Pooled		
				Amt.	%	Amt.	% FX	% Gold	%	FX	Gold
Core EU											
Germany	22.6	68.6	35.1	14.0	(20.4)	7.0	(10.2)	(19.9)	(13.5)	9.3	4.7
France	17.0	16.9	30.2	10.6	(62.5)	5.3	(31.2)	(17.5)	(22.4)	3.8	6.8
Netherlands	4.3	21.5	12.8	2.6	(12.3)	1.3	(6.1)	(10.3)	(7.7)	1.7	1.0
Belg/Lux'bg	3.0	14.2	5.7	1.8	(12.9)	0.9	(6.5)	(16.1)	(9.2)	1.3	0.5
Austria	2.3	21.0	4.0	1.4	(6.8)	0.7	(3.4)	(17.9)	(5.7)	1.2	0.2
Subtotal	49.1	142.2	87.8	30.5	(21.4)	15.2	(10.7)	(17.3)	(13.2)	18.8	11.6
Other EU											
Italy	15.9	39.0	24.6	9.8	(25.2)	4.9	(12.6)	(20.0)	(15.5)	6.0	3.8
U.K.	15.4	35.7	6.8	9.5	(26.7)	4.8	(13.4)	(70.1)	(22.4)	8.0	1.5
Spain	8.9	54.7	5.8	5.5	(10.0)	2.7	(5.0)	(47.4)	(9.1)	5.0	0.5
Sweden	2.9	17.8	1.8	1.8	(10.1)	0.9	(5.1)	(50.0)	(9.2)	1.6	0.2
Greece	2.0	17.0	1.3	1.2	(7.3)	0.6	(3.7)	(47.8)	(6.8)	1.2	0.0
Portugal	1.9	14.2	5.7	1.1	(8.1)	0.6	(4.0)	(10.1)	(5.8)	0.8	0.3
Denmark	1.7	13.3	0.6	1.1	(7.9)	0.5	(4.0)	(88.0)	(7.6)	1.0	0.0
Finland	1.7	6.1	0.6	1.0	(16.8)	0.5	(8.4)	(85.4)	(15.3)	0.9	0.0
Ireland	0.8	7.7	0.1	0.5	(6.5)	0.2	(3.2)	(248.4)	(6.4)	0.5	0.0
Subtotal	51.0	205.5	47.3	31.6	(15.4)	15.8	(7.7)	(33.4)	(12.5)	25.7	5.9
Total EU	100.0	347.7	135.1	62.1		31.1				44.6	17.5

SOURCES: IMF; BIS and author's estimates.

NOTE: Weights are taken from EMI, *Annual Report 1994*, p. 71. Components are rounded and may not sum to totals. At the end of 1996, one ECU was worth $1.242.

[a] Foreign-exchange (FX) reserves are calculated as total FX reserves at end of 1996 as reported by the IMF *less* one-fifth of gold reserves (at end-September), assumed to have been swapped for official ECUs.

[b] Market values at end of 1996.

As matters stand, therefore, European central banks are more likely to buy dollars for the purpose of maintaining reserve holdings than for the purpose of pooling. Given the market attention paid to their actions, however, shifts by any European central bank out of marks into dollars are likely to remain modest. Moreover, European central banks not involved in the initial union, but with commitments under an ERM II, could desire more marks and be prepared to buy some off-market.

Excess Dollars in the Long Run?

After monetary union, European central banks may find that they have more dollars than they need. Emerson et al. (1992) put the excess of reserves at between \$200 and \$230 billion, but Kenen (1995, p. 115) shows that such figures imply excess *dollar* holdings of something like \$40 to \$70 billion. Gros and Thygesen (1992, p. 254) use U.S. reserves as a benchmark to suggest excess reserves of about ECU 50 billion at one point in their discussion (p. 254) but swing back past the question further on and use unpooled reserves to suggest excess reserves of ECU 80 billion (p. 403).[60] The excess of reserves over each country's share of the ECU 50 billion (Table C–2) cannot be taken as the measure of this surplus, however, because calls beyond the ECU 50 billion can be made in the future. Unpooled reserves left at the national central banks, moreover, are not necessarily useless. Some countries, including Austria, Belgium, and Italy, have dollar debt outstanding. Furthermore, national central banks could conceivably carry out foreign-exchange intervention as long as they act "under instructions from the ECB."[61]

One crude but very popular benchmark against which to measure the potential excess is the shrinkage of EU members' international trade by about 60 percent when intra-EU trade ceases to be international. The fraction of EU members' trade with each other, however, is shrinking because their trade is expanding most rapidly (albeit from a low base) with fast-growing countries whose currencies are anchored to the dollar. One can imagine that EU countries would desire to reduce their international-reserve holdings by something like one-half. But it should be recalled that EU reserve holdings denominated in core EU currencies amount to one-third of total holdings. If this fraction of international reserves is allowed to become euro-denominated assets, EU countries will already have lost one-third of their total reserves. Given this potential for passive reserve reduction, active reserve management in Europe might yield a reduction of one-sixth in current reserves, or about \$55 billion.[62] Most analyses of this question by economists at banks and securities firms have taken something like this approach (Table C–3).

---

[60] Could the inconsistency have arisen from different treatments of the dollars "swapped" for official ECUs, more a nominal than a substantial transaction?

[61] See EMI (1996, p. 56), based on Article 31 of the ESCB/ECB Statute requiring ECB authorization for the foreign-exchange operations by national central banks.

[62] Golden (1996) and Parsons (1996) report different numbers using this same trade benchmark, whereas Brookes (1996) uses current ratios of reserves to imports for individual EU countries in recognition of the wide range of observed ratios: from 0.8 months' imports for France, through 3.4 for the EU on average, to a high of 7.0 for Greece. Keating's (1996) approach has much to recommend it. He uses the United States as a benchmark but measures U.S. reserves against U.S. trade with the nondollar area.

TABLE C-3
SURPLUS FOREIGN-EXCHANGE RESERVES OF EURO AREA: VARIOUS RECENT ESTIMATES
(*in billions of U.S. dollars*)

Source	Core EU	Other EU	Total EU	Benchmark
		Surplus		
CS First Boston (Keating, 1996)			None	Ratio of U.S. reserves to trade with nondollar area
JP Morgan (Persaud and Dambassinas, 1996)			30–70	Average ratio of reserves to imports for 23 industrial countries
Goldman Sachs (Brookes, 1996)	30	93	123	1994 ratios of reserves to imports for individual EU countries
Paribas (Parsons, 1996)			None	Current aggregate ratio of reserves to imports for the EU
Nomura (Golden, 1996)			100	Current aggregate ratio of reserves to imports for the EU
Union Bank of Switzerland (Adler and Chang, 1996)			Some reduction plausible	"Reserves are a residual that results from central banks leaning against the wind of dollar depreciation"
Salomon Brothers (Lipsky et al., 1996)			None	"In a world of free capital movements, trade flows are not a good guide to the desired scale of reserves"
Morgan Stanley (Bulchandani, 1997)			Possibly a deficit	Larger portfolio shifts with larger, more liquid euro financial markets
Deutsche Bank (Deutsch, 1997)	50–90	110–150	200	U.S. reserves equal to 1 to 1½ months imports
Deutsche Bank (Hoffman and Schröder, 1997)			130	U.S. reserves equal to 1 to 1½ months imports

NOTE: Estimates are presented in chronological order of appearance.

The trade benchmark is, however, an anachronism, a vestige of thinking from the Bretton Woods era, when capital controls made imports the first and often the last claim on reserves. When the Bank of England was mobilizing its reserves to defend the pound's link to the mark in September 1992, it was not only U.K. importers on the other side of the market. Imports range from one-tenth to one-third of GDP, but capital flows far exceed GDP (Table C–4).

In practice, central banks accumulate and hold reserves as much as a by-product of other policies as a product of reserve policy per se. Fritz Machlup's likening of reserve size and composition to the contents of his wife's closet—a collection of by-products of decisions rather than the object of an independent optimization—suffers more from changing social norms for acceptable images among economists than from its loss in truth value. A recent attempt to model European reserve holdings, done under genteel duress, produced little in the way of robust results (Leahy, 1997). Contrary to the assertions of some market analyses,[63] reserves are not expensive to hold for countries with good credit ratings. Even if surplus reserves can in some sense be identified, is it safe to presume that they will be sold?[64] Moreover, caution would suggest deferring any paring of reserves until the process of monetary union is very far advanced and the credibility of the ECB is well secured. These considerations, in combination with the amounts involved and the time horizon, suggest that any reserve liquidation will prove to be modest in scale and limited in effect.

TABLE C–4

CROSS-BORDER TRANSACTIONS IN BONDS AND EQUITIES
(*as a percentage of GDP*)

Country	1975	1980	1985	1989	1990	1991	1992	1993	1994	1995	1996
United States	4	9	35	101	89	96	107	129	131	135	163
Japan	2	8	62	156	119	92	72	78	60	65	84[a]
Germany	5	7	33	66	57	55	85	170	158	172	200
France	n.a.	5	21	52	54	79	122	187	197	187	228
Italy	1	1	4	18	27	60	92	192	207	253	468
Canada	3	10	27	55	64	81	113	153	212	194	258

SOURCE: National data.
NOTE: Figures represent gross purchases and sales of securities between residents and nonresidents as a percentage of GDP.
[a] Based on settlement data.

[63] "Excess reserves represent an economic loss," according to Persaud and Dambassinas (1996, p. 2).
[64] Kenen (1995, p. 114) notes that "the EC countries may be stuck with redundant dollars, just as they were stuck with gold after it was demonetized officially by the Second Amendment to the Articles of Agreement of the IMF." (European central banks could easily take a different view of gold acquired at $35 dollars an ounce, although total returns on dollars and gold measured from a late-1960s base have been converging for some time.)

Appendix D: European Monetary Union and the Structure of the Foreign-Exchange Market

It is a commonplace that monetary union in Europe will shrink turnover in the global foreign-exchange market. A euro area embracing all of the EU countries will deprive foreign-exchange dealers of something like 10 percent of their transactions (see Table 5 and BIS, 1997b, p. 92).[65] From the standpoint of the participants in the foreign-exchange market (if not from a broader point of view), this contraction of volume threatens to arrive at an awkward time. Technical change is already squeezing the revenue of market participants. Initially, electronic brokering offered by Reuters and a consortium of banks was meant to challenge the business of the voice brokers. But medium-sized banks that previously transacted directly with other banks have seen how electronic brokering has rendered price discovery in the market more transparent and has narrowed trading margins, and they, too, are switching away from direct dealing to electronic brokering. (At this stage, the innovation of electronic brokering appears to be on the steepening portion of its logistic S-curve of diffusion.)

Less well appreciated is the effect of the euro on the structure of foreign-exchange dealing. As things stand, the dollar remains the main vehicle currency in the foreign-exchange market. Although U.S. GDP and trade represent only one-fifth of the GDP and trade of industrial countries, the dollar is used on one side of over 80 percent of all transactions. The decline in the dollar's role as a vehicle currency has not favored a whole matrix of cross-exchange rates not involving the dollar, as modeled by Black (1991). Instead, it has favored the mark, which, as noted in this essay, is to be found on one side of $140 billion of the daily $150 billion in transactions of one EU currency against another. (Table 4 shows $300 billion of transactions in EMS currencies, but this figure counts both sides of each transaction, whereas the mark figure above counts only one side.) Thus, not only is a transaction of French francs against Spanish pesetas likely to entail transactions against marks, but a customer transaction of French francs against dollars is likely to be balanced with a franc/mark transaction and a dollar/mark transaction between interbank counterparties.

---

[65] This estimate is not much different from estimates made by Hartmann (1996) and Lipsky et al. (1996), which is not surprising considering that all estimates start with the *Central Bank Survey 1995* (BIS, 1996a).

Judging from the 1995 data, the euro, at its birth, will trade on a foreign-exchange market in which the dollar is more dominant than today. With a broad monetary union, the euro will appear on one side of 56 percent of all foreign-exchange transactions, larger than the 34 to 40 percent share of the mark, but smaller than the 70 percent share of EU currencies. The dollar will be on one side for nine out of ten dollars in foreign-exchange transactions, a fraction not observed since 1989 (BIS, 1993, pp. 8–9). Exchanges of euros against yen will amount to one-twentieth of exchanges of euros against dollars and one-tenth of exchanges of yen against dollars. The other sizable exchange-rate pair not involving the dollar will be exchanges of euros against Swiss francs, which might exceed one-third of transactions of dollars against Swiss francs.

Of course, a smaller euro area would leave more trading of euros against "out" currencies, perhaps the British pound and the Swedish krona. Hartmann (1996, pp. 21–22) notes that of the noncore European countries, only the United Kingdom would make a material difference to the structure of the foreign-exchange market by choosing not to adopt the euro. Still, the point would remain that the euro will start off as much less a vehicle currency than the mark, which is another way of saying that the mark's use as a vehicle currency has been largely confined to exchanges involving its neighbors' and near-neighbors' currencies.

It is plausible that the mark is developing into, and that the euro will become, the main means of exchange against the Eastern European currencies. Transactions in these currencies are at present small—over $6 billion per day (Table D–1)—smaller than 1995 transactions between the mark and the guilder, ECU, krona, peseta, or lira. Nevertheless, the question is interesting insofar as transactions in these currencies are likely to grow rapidly. Table D–2 suggests that, except in the Czech Republic, dollar transactions tend to exceed mark transactions against local currencies on the local foreign-exchange markets in Eastern Europe. Although the mark is probably serving as a vehicle for transactions between other core European currencies and these emerging currencies, it is not obvious that the mark is serving as a vehicle for transactions involving currencies outside Europe.

Thus, the euro stands to incorporate most of the currencies for which the mark plays a vehicle role at present. "The potential of the euro to become a forex vehicle for the rest of the world" could start out as pure potential (Hartmann, 1996, p. 23).

TABLE D–1

FOREIGN-EXCHANGE TURNOVER IN EMERGING CURRENCIES

(in billions of U.S. dollars)

Currency	Local Turnover[a]		Global Turnover		
	April 1995	April 1996	March 1996[b]	April 1997[b]	Early 1996[c]
Asia	>13.6	>17.8	>16.3	>39.4	36.6
Indian rupee	1.6[d]	1.2	1.0	n.a.	1.1
Indonesian rupiah	4.8[d]	7.8[d]	3.5	10.0	8.5
Korean won	3.1	3.2	1.8	2.4	2.4
Malaysian ringgit	n.a.	n.a.	5.0	10.0	9.5
New Taiwan dollar	1.5	1.6	n.a.	3.0	1.1
Thai baht	2.6[d]	4.0[d]	5.0	14.0	14.0
Latin America	9.1	10.9	>5.8	n.a.	
Argentine peso	1.7	2.0	n.a.	1.5	
Brazilian real	4.3[e]	5.5[e]	4.5	n.a.	
Chilean peso	0.8	0.9	n.a.	n.a.	
Colombian peso	0.1[d]	0.1[d]	0.1	n.a.	
New Mexican peso	2.1	2.2	1.2	n.a.	
New Peruvian sol	0.1	0.2	n.a.	n.a.	
Eastern Europe	1.8	>5.9	>1.6	8.1	
Czech koruna	0.6[d]	2.5[d]	0.5	5.5	
Hungarian forint	0.3	0.6	0.3	0.4	
Polish zloty	0.3[d]	n.a.	0.3	0.35	
Russian ruble	0.6	2.6	0.5	1.4	
Slovak koruna	0.02	0.2	n.a.	0.4	
Other currencies	5.4	6.7	>7.4	>7.0	
New Israeli shekel	0.3	0.5	n.a.	n.a.	
Saudi riyal	1.4	1.5	0.3	n.a.	
South African rand	3.7	4.7	6.0	6.0	
Turkish lira	0.01[d]	0.02[d]	1.1	1.0	
Total[f]	>29.9	>41.3	>31.1	>56.0	

SOURCES: Citibank; Singapore Foreign Exchange Market Committee, *Annual Report 1996*; BIS, *Central Bank Survey 1995*; national central banks.

NOTE: The countries shown (except South Africa) had an aggregate GDP of $3.4 trillion in 1992, or 15 percent of world GDP, compared to 80 percent for the countries included in the April 1995 *Central Bank Survey*.

[a] Unless otherwise specified, figures are estimates reported by the respective central banks, net of double-counting, for a period as near as possible to April. For Thailand, figures are 1995 second-half and 1996 annual averages. For Indonesia and Argentina, they are annual averages. The turnover of the Russian ruble and the South African rand was well above the annual average in April.

[b] Citibank estimates, net of double-counting.

[c] Estimates reported in Singapore Foreign Exchange Market Committee, *Annual Report 1996*.

[d] On a gross basis.

[e] Includes other currencies.

[f] The *Central Bank Survey 1995* reports a grand total (including South Africa) of $1,136.9 billion.

TABLE D-2

TURNOVER IN EMERGING CURRENCIES, BY CURRENCY IN APRIL 1996
(in millions of dollars)

Currency	Dollar	Mark	Yen	Total
Eastern Europe	4,786	1,920	48	7,161
Czech koruna[a]	1,025	1,421	0	2,532
Hungarian forint	334	105	35	626
Polish zloty	863	270	0	1,174
Slovak koruna	117	71	12[b]	200
Asia	10,090	78	145	10,498
Indian rupee	1,104	38	11	1,214
Korean won	3,082	13	50	3,180
New Taiwan dollar	1,924	20	69	2,090
Thai baht[c]	3,980	7	15	4,014
Other currencies	6,286	>143	>99	6,690
New Israeli shekel	385	n.a.	n.a.	469
Saudi riyal	1,410	3	3	1,494
South African rand	4,470	140	96	4,706
Turkish lira[a]	21	0	0	21

SOURCES: National central banks.

NOTE: In some cases, the total includes transactions not involving domestic currency and thus does not match the local turnover shown in Table D-1.

[a] On a gross basis.

[b] All other.

[c] Annual average, on a gross basis.

Appendix E: Currency Invoicing of International Trade

The importance of the currency invoicing of international trade is easily overstated. There was a time when the unit of account for international trade, one of the functions of international money, could be strongly related to the means-of-payment function, as measured by turnover in the foreign-exchange market. But these days, when world trade turns over in the global foreign-exchange market twice a week, this relationship has lost its strength.[66]

[66] After monetary union, trade will represent something like 10 percent of GDP for the euro area, the United States, and Japan. By contrast, the international bond and equity flows, alone, exceed GDP for major countries, in some cases by sizable multiples (Table C-4). Contrary to the assumption of Black (1991, p. 522), the denomination of trade can no longer be taken to have much of a direct effect on the use of different currencies in the foreign-exchange market.

What does the contractual currency tell us? If exports are priced in dollars, does that mean that private or official external borrowing in foreign currency ultimately secured by these exports should likewise be denominated in dollars? The question as usually posed misses the distinction between what might be called the nominal or apparent currency of denomination and the effective currency of denomination. The case of gold illustrates this distinction. The gold trade has all along been conducted in dollars. Yet the response of the dollar price of gold to changes in the dollar/mark exchange rate fifteen years ago suggests that the price of gold at that time was effectively set more in marks than in dollars. In contrast, the comparative lack of such an exchange-rate response these days suggests that gold is now truly priced in dollars, not only in appearance, but also in substance. Under these circumstances, it would have made more sense some years ago than it would today for South Africa to borrow abroad in European currencies and to manage the rand against those currencies. The invoicing of exports of gold offered no clue.

As noted by the Bundesbank (1991, p. 43), moreover, a substantial fraction of the invoicing, especially that of trade in manufactures, reflects the pricing of transactions between wholly owned affiliates of the same firm, the invoicing decisions of which may reflect accounting, tax, or organizational choices.

Not only is the question of the denomination of international trade often misapprehended, but the data are poor. The very useful effort by the European Commission (Ilzkovitz, 1995) to bring together data from the United States, Japan, Germany, France, the United Kingdom, Italy, and the Netherlands confronted the fact that little information is available on the portion of world trade that is growing most rapidly, that is, trade among developing and emerging countries. Table E–1 is derived from this effort, but its limitations must be understood. The invoicing of trade among Asian countries other than Japan is estimated using Japanese data, and trade among Latin American countries is taken to be a mix of U.S. and European behavior (with two-third and one-third weights). The danger in these quite understandable estimation methods is that the dollar's share may be underrepresented. More important, the information gap implies that we do not really know how invoicing behavior is evolving over time.

All that said, it appears that there are some fairly robust observations. Only the dollar is used extensively as a vehicle currency in the strict sense, that is, to denominate trade between two other countries. For the big industrial countries, the bulk of exports tends to be invoiced in the

INVOICING OF INTERNATIONAL TRADE BY CURRENCY
(in billions of U.S. dollars and percentage of exports)

Currency	1980 %	1987 %	1992 World	%	Intra-EU	%	Extra-EU	%
U.S. dollar	(56)	(48)	1,741	(48)	141	(4)	1,599	(59)
Major EU currencies	(31)	(34)	1,225	(34)	627	(17)	598	(22)
German mark	(14)	(16)	559	(15)	297	(8)	263	(10)
French franc	(6)	(7)	230	(6)	117	(3)	114	(4)
Dutch guilder	(3)	(3)	102	(3)	48	(1)	54	(2)
Italian lira	(2)	(3)	124	(3)	62	(2)	62	(2)
British pound	(7)	(6)	208	(6)	103	(3)	105	(4)
Japanese yen	(2)	(4)	176	(5)	4	(0)	171	(6)
Total global exports	(100)	(100)	3,656	(100)			2,693	(100)
Memorandum:								
Estimated EU-15							679	(25)

SOURCES: Hartmann, "The Future of the Euro," 1996, p. 7 (citing Ilzkovitz, 1995); United Nations (for trade data).

home currency, although this has become less true over time, with nine-tenths of U.S. exports being invoiced in dollars but less than half of Japanese exports being invoiced in yen.[67] This invoicing difference between the United States and other industrial countries is consistent with studies of effective pricing behavior that find that U.S. export prices reflect domestic prices, whereas exporters to the United States show some tendency to price to the U.S. market. Industrial-country imports tend to be more dollar-denominated than their exports, reflecting the importance of commodity imports. As matters stood in the early 1990s, the dollar's share of trade invoicing was near one-half (Table E–1); its decline since 1980 seems due to the decline in the share of oil trade (Bundesbank, 1991, p. 42; Ilzkovitz, 1995, p. 71).

The advent of the euro will presumably lead to less use of the dollar to denominate intra-European trade. Whether the dollar will be supplanted in all its uses—for instance, to denominate energy exports from the Netherlands and the United Kingdom to Germany (Bundesbank,

[67] Kenen (1983, p. 9 and table 4) notes, by contrast, that exports from industrial countries generally came to be invoiced to a greater extent in the home currency—at the expense of the dollar—between 1972 and 1976. Kenen's explanation, "the increase of uncertainty attending the change in the exchange-rate regime," would not have predicted the recent reversal of the earlier trend.

1991, p. 42)—remains to be seen.[68] But putting aside this question, one can calculate invoicing shares on the hypothesis of a broad monetary union using 1992 data on global invoicing practices. The decline in the use of the euro relative to major EU currencies—from 34 percent of world trade to 22 percent—can be seen as a mechanical, arithmetic, or even misleading, result of the reclassification of intra-EU trade as domestic (which, however one feels about it on analytic grounds, is increasingly hard to avoid, given the effect of open borders on European statistics). Alternatively, the potential reduction in the use of European currencies might be seen as a result of the largely regional importance of the deutsche mark at present.

One can summarize the observations by noting that in 1992, the dollar was used to denominate trade 3.6 times the value of U.S. trade, whereas the corresponding intensity for the mark was 1.4, for the French franc and British pound, about 1, and for the yen, lira, and guilder, between 0.6 and 0.8. Under the assumption of monetary union, the euro would start off with an intensity of about 1, much like the franc or pound today. Even this figure may be overstated in that it assumes that intra-European trade is not more intensively denominated in European currencies than is extra-European trade (Hartmann, 1996), an assumption not justified by the Bundesbank data.

Looking forward, some analysts attempt to arrive at a reasonable role for the euro in trade invoicing by suggesting that the euro can be expected to rise to an intensity of 1.4, much as the mark has today (Persaud and Dambassinas, 1996). This seems modest on its face, but on closer examination, it is not so innocent. As noted above, the mark does not figure importantly in contracts between third countries. Its high use in international trade relative to German trade reflects its dominance on both sides of German trade with Western Europe—77 percent of German exports and 53 percent of German imports (Issing, 1996, p. 6).[69] Less than half of German imports from other countries are denominated in marks. To assume that the euro will rise to an intensity of 1.4, therefore, is to posit that the area of heavy euro use will be as large relative to the euro area as Western Europe is to Germany. For the reasons sketched above in Section 4, the outlook for such a development is by no means certain.

[68] Contrast Alogoskoufis and Portes (1992, p. 281), who state that "the dollar will certainly be displaced in intra-EC trade as a result of . . . monetary union."

[69] The figures have fallen from 80 and 60 percent, respectively, in the 1990s; see Deutsche Bundesbank, 1991, p. 42.

Some analysts have tried to reason from prospects for the use of the euro in the invoicing of trade to portfolio shifts by private investors. But more trade invoiced in euros would entail not only more holdings of bank accounts denominated in euros with which to effect payments but also more borrowing in euros as the euro-denominated trade paper is discounted. Thus, the change in investor preferences or habits as a result of the greater invoicing of trade in euros needs to be large to represent a net demand for euro assets.

In summary, much less is known about invoicing behavior than one would like. Moreover, much of what little is known about trade invoicing is not well understood; many conclusions drawn from invoicing practices regarding economic exposure to exchange-rate changes suffer from the fallacy of misplaced concreteness. And the euro should not be expected quickly to serve as large a role in invoicing in relation to the euro area's trade as the mark did in relation to Germany's trade, because the mark's outsized role is the flip side of the relatively small invoicing role played by the currencies of Germany's neighbors.

References

Adler, Oliver, and Kelly Chang, "The Myth of an EMU-Related Reserve Sell-Off," Union Bank of Switzerland, *UBS Global Research—Currencies*, November 26, 1996.

Alogoskoufis, George, and Richard Portes, "International Costs and Benefits from EMU," *European Economy*, Special Edition No. 1, Pt. 5 (1991), pp. 231–245.

———, "European Monetary Union and International Currencies in a Tripolar World," in Matthew B. Canzoneri, Vittorio Grilli, and Paul R. Masson, eds., *Establishing a Central Bank: Issues in Europe and Lessons from the US*, Cambridge and New York, Cambridge University Press, 1992, pp. 273–300.

———, "The Euro, the Dollar and the International Monetary System," in Paul R. Masson, Thomas H. Krueger, and Bart G. Turtelboom, eds., *EMU and the International Monetary System*, Washington, D.C., International Monetary Fund, 1997, pp. 58–89.

Alogoskoufis, George, Richard Portes, and Hélène Rey, "The Emergence of the Euro as an International Currency," paper presented to the 26th Panel Meeting of Economic Policy, Bonn, October 17–18, 1997; forthcoming in *Economic Policy*.

Alzola, José Luis, "Euro Won't Trigger Drop of Dollar," Salomon Brothers, *EMU and the Euro*, Economic and Market Analysis, May 16, 1997.

Arrowsmith, John, and Christopher Taylor, *Unresolved Issues on the Way to a Single Currency*, Occasional Paper No. 49, London, National Institute of Economic and Social Research, 1996.

Artus, Patrick, "A Strong Euro or a Weak Euro," Working Paper No. 1996–02EI, Caisse des Dépôts et Consignations, Service des Études Économiques et Financières, November 1996.

Backé, Peter, and Isabella Lindner, "European Monetary Union: Prospects for EU Member States and Selected Candidate Countries from Central and Eastern Europe," in Oesterreichische Nationalbank, *Focus on Transition*, 2, Vienna, 1996, pp. 20–40.

Bank for International Settlements (BIS), *Central Bank Survey of Foreign Exchange Market Activity in April 1992*, Basle, Bank for International Settlements, March 1993.

———, *Central Bank Survey of Foreign Exchange and Derivatives Market Activity 1995*, Basle, Bank for International Settlements, May 1996a.

———, *66th Annual Report*, Basle, Bank for International Settlements, 1996b.

———, *International Banking and Financial Market Developments*, Basle, Bank for International Settlements, May 1997a.

———, *67th Annual Report*, Basle, Bank for International Settlements, 1997b.

———, *Handbook on Central Banks of Central and Eastern Europe*, June 1997c.

Baumol, William J., "The Transactions Demand for Cash: An Inventory Theoretic Approach," *Quarterly Journal of Economics*, 66 (November 1952), pp. 545–556; reprinted in Thomas Mayer, ed., *Monetary Theory*, International Library of Critical Writings in Economics, No. 7, Aldershot, U.K., and Brookfield, Vt., Edward Elgar, 1990, pp. 3–14.

Begg, David K., Francesco Giavazzi, and Charles Wyplosz, "Options for the Future Exchange Rate Policy of the EMU," Report prepared by CEPR for the Directorate-General for Economic and Financial Affairs of the European Commission, 2nd draft, July 3, 1997, processed.

Bénassy-Quéré, Agnès, "Exchange Rate Regimes and Policies in Asia," Working Paper No. 96–07, Paris, Centre d'Études Prospectives et d'Informations Internationales (CEPII), July 1996a.

———, "Potentialities and Opportunities of the Euro as an International Currency" Economic Papers No. 115, Brussels, Commission of the European Communities, July 1996b.

Bénassy-Quéré, Agnès, Benoit Mojon, and Jean Pisani-Ferry, "The Euro and Exchange Rate Stability," in Paul R. Masson, Thomas H. Krueger, and Bart G. Turtelboom, eds., *EMU and the International Monetary System*, Washington, D.C., International Monetary Fund, 1997, pp. 157–193.

Bergsten, C. Fred, "The Impact of the Euro on Exchange Rates and International Policy Cooperation," in Paul R. Masson, Thomas H. Krueger, and Bart G. Turtelboom, eds., *EMU and the International Monetary System*, Washington, D.C., International Monetary Fund, 1997, pp. 17–48.

Berrigan, John, and Hervé Carré, "Exchange Arrangements between the EU and Countries in Eastern Europe, the Mediterranean, and the CFA Zone," in Paul R. Masson, Thomas H. Krueger, and Bart G. Turtelboom, eds., *EMU and the International Monetary System*, Washington, D.C., International Monetary Fund, 1997, pp. 122–135.

Black, Stanley, "Transactions Costs and Vehicle Currencies," *Journal of International Money and Finance*, 10 (December 1991), pp. 512–526.

Borensztein, Eduardo, and Carmen M. Reinhart, "The Macroeconomic Determinants of Commodity Prices," *International Monetary Fund Staff Papers*, 41 (June 1994), pp. 236–261.

Borio, Claudio E.V., and Robert N. McCauley, "The Anatomy of the Bond Market Turbulence of 1994," in Franco Bruni, Donald E. Fair, and Richard O'Brien, eds., *Risk Management in Volatile Financial Markets*, Dordrecht and Boston, Kluwer, on behalf of the Société Universitaire Européenne de Recherches Financières, 1996a, pp. 61–84.

——, *The Economics of Recent Bond Yield Volatility*, BIS Economic Papers No. 45, Basle, Bank for International Settlements, July 1996b.

Branson, William, and Dale Henderson, "The Specification and Influence of Asset Markets," in Ronald W. Jones and Peter B. Kenen, eds., *Handbook of International Economics*, Vol. 2, Amsterdam and New York, North-Holland, Elsevier, 1985, pp. 749–805.

Brookes, Martin, "EMU's Excess Foreign Reserves," Goldman Sachs European Economics Analyst, *EMU Briefing*, No. 6, September 4, 1996.

Brown, Brendan, *The Dollar/Mark Axis*, London, Macmillan, 1979.

——, *The Economics of the Swap Market*, Routledge, London, 1989.

Buiter, Willem H., Giancarlo M. Corsetti, and Paolo A. Pesenti, *Financial Markets and Internal Monetary Cooperation: The Lessons of the 92–93 ERM Crisis*, Cambridge and New York, Cambridge University Press, forthcoming 1997.

Bulchandani, Ravi, "More on the Euro as a Reserve Currency," Morgan Stanley Investment Research—U.K. and Europe, *EMU Insights*, March 7, 1997, pp. 10–12.

Cantor, Richard, and Frank Packer, "Determinants and Impact of Sovereign Credit Ratings," *Federal Reserve Bank of New York Economic Policy Review*, 2 (October 1996), pp. 37–53.

Chen, Edward K.Y. (President, Lingnan College), "Hong Kong beyond 1997: Economic and Financial Issues," keynote address to the Conference on Asia, Europe, and America in a New Global Environment: A Challenge to Liberal Visions for the Next Century, sponsored by the Friedrich Naumann Foundation in cooperation with Lingnan College, Hong Kong, January 19, 1997.

Clarida, Richard, Jordi Gali, and Mark Gertler, "Monetary Policy Rules in Practice: Some International Evidence," paper presented to the European Summer Institute, Berlin, September 10–13, 1997.

Clarke, Ian, and Clive Parry, "EMU—Plan B," in *EMU Countdown: 682 Days to Go*, Morgan Stanley Fixed Income Portfolio Strategy, February 18, 1997.

Cohen, Daniel, "How Will the Euro Behave?" in Paul R. Masson, Thomas H. Krueger, and Bart G. Turtelboom, eds., *EMU and the International Monetary System*, Washington, D.C., International Monetary Fund, 1997, pp. 397–497.

Commission for Economic Issues, Subcommittee on EMU [for Switzerland], "Switzerland Face to Economic and Monetary Union in Europe: An Analysis of the Economic Aspects," Summary in English of report to the Committee for General Economic Policy of the Federal Council, Berne, Federal Office for Economic Policy, August 1996.

Commission of the European Communities (European Commission), "Draft Paper on the Technical Preparations of the Bond Markets," Luxembourg, Consultative Group on the Impact of the Introduction of the Euro on Capital Markets [Giovanninni Group], March 1997a.

———, "External Aspects of Economic and Monetary Union," Staff Working Paper SEC(97) 803, Luxembourg, Commission of the European Communities, April 23, 1997b.

Consensus Economics, Inc., *Consensus Forecasts*, August 1996, August 1997.

Dammers, Clifford R., "Should a Single Currency Mean Harmonisation of Market Conventions?" presentation to the Government Borrowers' Forum, Dublin, May 12, 1997.

Davies, Gavyn, "What If EMU Were Postponed?" Goldman Sachs European Economics Analyst, *EMU Briefing*, No. 5, February 28, 1997.

de Boissieu, Christian, "Stability in a Multiple Reserve Asset System," in Michael Mussa, James M. Boughton, and Peter Isard, eds., *The Future of the SDR in Light of Changes in the International Financial System*, Washington, D.C., International Monetary Fund, 1996, pp. 122–144.

De Grauwe, Paul, "Forward Interest Rates as Predictors of EMU," CEPR Discussion Paper No. 1395, London, Centre for Economic Policy Research, May 1996a.

———, "Reforming the Transition to EMU," in Peter B. Kenen, ed., *Making EMU Happen: Problems and Proposals: A Symposium*, Essays in International Finance No. 199, Princeton, N.J., Princeton University, International Finance Section, August 1996b.

———, "Exchange Rate Arrangements between the Ins and the Outs," in Paul R. Masson, Thomas H. Krueger, and Bart G. Turtelboom, eds., *EMU and the International Monetary System*, Washington, D.C., International Monetary Fund, 1997, pp. 97–118.

Deutsch, Klaus Günter, "EMU and Reserve Management at European Central Banks—Consequences and Unanswered Questions," Deutsche Bank Research, *EMU Watch*, No. 29, March 12, 1997.

Deutsche Bundesbank, "The Significance of the Deutsche Mark as an Invoicing Currency in Foreign Trade," *Monthly Report of Deutsche Bundesbank*, 43 (November 1991), pp. 40–44.

———, "The Circulation of Deutsche Mark Abroad," *Monthly Report of the Deutsche Bundesbank*, 47 (July 1995), pp. 65–71.

———, "The Role of the Deutsche Mark as International Investment and Reserve Currency," *Monthly Report of the Deutsche Bundesbank*, 49 (April 1997), pp. 17–30.

"Dispute over ESCB Profits," *Central Banking*, 6 (Spring 1997), pp. 7–10.

Domanski, Dietrich, and Holger Neuhaus, "Bond Market Volatility in Germany," in *Financial Market Volatility*, BIS Conference Papers No. 1, Basle, Bank for International Settlements, March 1996, pp. 113–128.

Dooley, Michael J., Saul Lizondo, and Donald J. Mathieson, "The Currency Composition of Foreign Exchange Reserves," *International Monetary Fund Staff Papers*, 36, June 1989, pp. 385–434.

Dornbusch, Rudiger, Carlo Favero, and Francesco Giavazzi, paper presented to the 26th Panel Meeting of Economic Policy, Bonn, October 17–18, 1997; forthcoming in *Economic Policy*.

Dornbusch, Rudiger, "Policy and Performance Links between LDC Debtors and Industrial Nations," *Brookings Papers in Economic Activity*, No. 2 (1985), pp. 303–368.

Dupont, Dominique, and V. Hugo Juan-Ramon, "Real Exchange Rates and Commodity Prices," International Monetary Fund Working Paper No. 96/27, Washington, D.C., International Monetary Fund, April 1996.

Edison, Hali J., and Linda S. Kole, "European Monetary Arrangements: Implications for the Dollar, Exchange Rate Variability and Credibility," Board of Governors of the Federal Reserve System, *International Finance Discussion Papers*, No. 468, Washington, D.C., May 1994.

Eichengreen, Barry, *Should the Maastricht Treaty Be Saved?* Princeton Studies in International Finance No. 74, Princeton, N.J., Princeton University, International Finance Section, December 1992.

Eichengreen, Barry, and Tamim Bayoumi, "Is Asia an Optimum Currency Area? Can It Become One? Regional, Global and Historical Perspectives on Asian Monetary Relations," Working Paper No. C96–081, Center for International and Development Economics Research, University of California, Berkeley, December 1996.

Eichengreen, Barry, and Jeffrey A. Frankel, "Implications of the Future Evolution of the International Monetary System" in Michael Mussa, James M. Boughton, and Peter Isard, eds., *The Future of the SDR in Light of Changes in the International Financial System*, Washington, D.C., International Monetary Fund, 1996, pp. 337–378.

Emerson, Michael, Daniel Gros, Alexander Italianer, Jean Pisani-Ferry, and Horst Reichenbach, *One Market, One Money: An Evaluation of the Potential Benefits and Costs of Forming an Economic and Monetary Union*, Oxford and New York, Oxford University Press, 1992.

Ettlin, Franz, "On the Fundamental Determinants of the Swiss Franc Exchange Rate for the D-Mark" in *The Determination of Long-Term Interest Rates and Exchange Rates and the Role of Expectations*, BIS Conference Papers No. 2, Basle, Bank for International Settlements, August 1996, pp. 18–27.

European Commission, see Commission of the European Communities.

European Monetary Institute (EMI), *Annual Report 1994*, Frankfurt, European Monetary Institute, April 1995.

——, *Annual Report 1995*, Frankfurt, European Monetary Institute, April 1996.

———, *Annual Report 1996*, Frankfurt, European Monetary Institute, April 1997.

Frankel, Jeffrey A., "The Implications of Mean-Variance Optimization for Four Questions in International Macroeconomics," *Journal of International Money and Finance*, 5 (March 1986), pp. 553–575.

———, "Still the Lingua Franca: The Exaggerated Death of the Dollar," *Foreign Affairs*, 74 (July-August 1995), pp. 9–16.

Frankel, Jeffrey A., and Shang-Jin Wei, "Trade Blocs and Currency Blocs," National Bureau of Economic Research Working Paper No. 4335, Cambridge, Mass., National Bureau of Economic Research, April 1993.

———, "Yen Bloc or Dollar Bloc? Exchange Rate Policies of the East Asian Economies," in Takatoshi Ito and Anne O. Krueger, eds., *Macroeconomic Linkage: Savings, Exchange Rates, and Capital Flows*, Chicago, University of Chicago Press, 1994, pp. 295–329.

Frenkel, Jacob A., and Morris Goldstein, "The International Role of the Deutsche Mark," in *Fifty Years of the Deutsche Mark*, Frankfurt, Deutsche Bundesbank, forthcoming 1997.

Funke, Norbert, and Michael Kennedy, "International Economic Implications of the Euro," *OECD Economic Outlook*, 61 (June 1997), pp. 24–30.

Galati, Gabriele, "Trade Links, Business Cycle Symmetries and Currency Links," Working Paper, Basle, Bank for International Settlements, forthcoming 1997.

Galati, Gabriele, and Robert N. McCauley, "Explaining the Dollar/Mark Polarity," Working Paper, Basle, Bank for International Settlements, forthcoming 1997.

Garber, Peter M., "The Use of the Yen as a Reserve Currency," Institute for Monetary and Economic Studies, Bank of Japan, *Monetary and Economic Studies*, 14 (December 1996), pp. 1–21.

Ghironi, Fabio, and Francesco Giavazzi, "Policy Implications of the Size of EMU for Europe and the United States," in Paul R. Masson, Thomas H. Krueger, and Bart G. Turtelboom, eds., *EMU and the International Monetary System*, Washington, D.C., International Monetary Fund, 1997, pp. 421–477.

Giavazzi, Francesco, and Alberto Giovannini, *Limiting Exchange Rate Flexibility*, Cambridge, Mass., MIT Press, 1989.

Golden, Chris, "The Effects of EMU on the Major Trade Currencies," Nomura Fixed Income Research, September 1996.

Group of Ten Deputies (G–10), *International Capital Movements and Foreign Exchange Markets: A Report to the Ministers and Governors*, Basle, Bank for International Settlements, April 1993.

Gros, Daniel, and Niels Thygesen, *European Monetary Integration: From the European Monetary System to European Monetary Union*, London, Longman, and New York, St. Martin's, 1992.

Hamada, Koichi, "Comment on 'Yen Bloc or Dollar Bloc?'" in Takatoshi Ito and Anne O. Krueger, eds., *Macroeconomic Linkage: Savings, Exchange Rates, and Capital Flows*, Chicago, University of Chicago Press, 1994, pp. 329–331.

Hartmann, Philipp, "The Future of the Euro as an International Currency: A Transactions Perspective," *Centre for European Policy Studies Research Report*, No. 20, (December 1996), pp. 1–28.

Heller, Robert, and Malcolm Knight, *Reserve-Currency Preferences of Central Banks*, Essays in International Finance No. 131, Princeton, N.J., Princeton University, International Finance Section, December 1978.

Hoffman, Ralf, and Ulrich Schröder, "The Euro—A Challenge to the Dollar?" Deutsche Bank Research, *EMU Watch*, No. 33, June 25, 1997.

Hong Kong Monetary Authority, *Annual Report 1996*, Hong Kong, Hong Kong Monetary Authority, 1997.

Honohan, Patrick, "The Break-Up of a Currency Union Increases the Demand for Money," *European Economic Review*, 25 (July 1984), pp. 235–238.

Hung, Juann, Charles Pigott, and Anthony Rodrigues, "Financial Implications of the U.S. External Deficit," *Federal Reserve Bank of New York Quarterly Review*, 13/14 (Winter/Spring 1989), pp. 33–51.

Icard, André, "Dollar, Deutschemark, Yen, Euro: Qu'est-Ce Qu'une Monnaie Internationale?" in André Cartapanis, ed., *Turbulences et Spéculations dans l'Économie Mondiale*, Paris, Economica, 1996, pp. 175–201.

Illmanen, Antii, "EMU Trades: Insights from Post-1999 Forward Rates," Salomon Brothers Economic and Market Analysis, *Euro Strategist*, May 21, 1997, pp. 18–22.

Ilzkovitz, Fabienne, "Recent Developments in the International Use of Currencies: Towards a Tripolar Regime?" in ECU Institute, ed., *International Currency Competition and the Future Role of the Single European Currency*, London and Boston, Kluwer Law International, 1995, pp. 67–95.

————, "Prospects for the Internationalization of the Euro," European Commission, June 1996, pp. 1–15, processed.

International Energy Agency, *World Energy Outlook*, Paris, International Energy Agency, 1996.

International Monetary Fund, *Exchange Arrangements and Exchange Restrictions, Annual Report*, Washington, D.C., International Monetary Fund, 1997.

Issing, Otmar, "Mögliche Auswirkungen der Europäischen Währungsunion auf die internationalen Finanzmärkte," speech before Internationalen Zins-Forum, Frankfurt, December 2, 1996, in Deutsche Bundesbank, *Auszüge aus Pressartikeln*, No. 76/6, December 1996.

Jeanneau, Serge, "Interest Rate Futures: Characteristics and Market Development" in Bank for International Settlements, *International Banking and Financial Market Developments*, November 1995 and February 1996.

Johnson, Christopher, *In with the Euro, Out with the Pound: The Single Currency for Britain*, London, Penguin, 1996.

Johnson, Karen H., "International Dimension of European Monetary Union: Implications for the Dollar," Board of Governors of the Federal Reserve System International Finance Discussion Paper No. 469, Washington, D.C., May 1994.

Keating, Giles, "Forex Reserves After EMU: Ample Dollars," Credit Suisse

First Boston, *Economics Research—Europe*, June 4, 1996.

Kenen, Peter B., *The Role of the Dollar as an International Currency*, Occasional Paper No. 13, New York, Group of Thirty, 1983.

——, *Economic and Monetary Union in Europe*, Cambridge, New York, and Melbourne, Cambridge University Press, 1995.

——, *Sorting Out Some EMU Issues*, Reprints in International Finance No. 29, Princeton, N.J., Princeton University, International Finance Section, December 1996.

——, "Preferences, Domains, and Sustainability," *American Economic Review*, 87 (May 1997), pp. 211–213.

Kindleberger, Charles P., *Balance-of-Payments Deficits and the International Market for Liquidity*, Essays in International Finance No. 46, Princeton, N.J., Princeton University, International Finance Section, May 1965.

——, "The Dollar Yesterday, Today and Tomorrow," *Banca Nazionale del Lavoro Quarterly Review*, 155 (December 1985), pp. 295–308.

——, *World Economic Primacy, 1500–1990*, New York, Oxford University Press, 1996.

Kindleberger, Charles P., with Emile Despres, and Walter Salant, "The Dollar and World Liquidity: a Minority View," *The Economist*, 218, No. 6389, February 5, 1966; reprinted in Kindleberger, *International Money*, London, Allen & Unwin, 1981, pp. 42–52.

King, Stephen, "European Monetary Union: Four Endings and a Funeral," London, HSBC James Capel Economics, 3rd quarter, 1996.

Koch, Elmar B., "Exchange Rates and Monetary Policy in Central Europe," *Most*, 7 (1997), pp. 1–48.

Koo, Richard C. "Japan and International Capital Flows," presentations to Nomura Central Bank Seminar, Tokyo, Nomura Research Institute, April 1992–1996.

Krugman, Paul, "The International Role of the Dollar: Theory and Prospect," in John F. O. Bilson and Richard C. Marston, eds., *Exchange Rate Theory and Practice*, Chicago, University of Chicago Press, 1984, pp. 261–278.

Kwan, C. H., *Economic Interdependence in the Asia-Pacific Region: Towards a Yen Bloc*, London and New York, Routledge, 1994.

Lascelles, David, "The Crash of 2003: An EMU Fairy Tale," No. 25, London, Centre for the Study of Financial Innovation, December 1996.

Laxton, Douglas, and Eswar Prasad, "Possible Effects of European Monetary Union on Switzerland: A Case Study of Policy Dilemmas Caused by Low Inflation and the Nominal Interest Rate Floor," International Monetary Fund Working Paper No. 97/23, Washington, D.C., International Monetary Fund, February 1997.

Leahy, Michael P., "The Dollar as an Official Reserve Currency under EMU," *Open Economies Review*, 7 (January 1997), pp. 371–390.

Lipsky, John, et al., *Managing Convergence: Market Implications for 1997 and Beyond*, Economic & Market Analysis, New York, Salomon Brothers, December 1996.

McCauley, Robert N., "Prospects for an Integrated European Government

Bond Market," in Bank for International Settlements, *International Banking and Financial Market Developments*, August 1996, pp. 18–31.

McCauley, Robert N., Frank Iacono, and Judith S. Rudd, *Dodging Bullets: Changing U.S. Corporate Capital Structures in the 1980s and 1990s*, Cambridge, Mass., MIT Press, forthcoming 1998.

McCauley, Robert N., and Will Melick, "Risk Reversal Risk," *Risk* (November 1996a), pp. 54–57.

————, "Propensity and Density," *Risk* (December 1996b), pp. 52–54.

McCauley, Robert N., and William R. White, "The Euro and European Financial Markets," in Paul R. Masson, Thomas H. Krueger, and Bart G. Turtelboom, eds., *EMU and the International Monetary System*, Washington, D.C., International Monetary Fund, 1997, pp. 324–388.

McCauley, Robert N., and Stephen Yeaple, "How Lower Japanese Asset Prices Affect Pacific Financial Markets," *Federal Reserve Bank of New York Quarterly Review*, 19 (Spring 1994), pp. 19–33.

Martin, Phillipe, "The Exchange Rate Policy of the Euro: A Matter of Size?" CEPR Discussion Paper No. 1646, London, Centre for Economic Policy Research, May 1997.

Masson, Paul R., and Bart G. Turtelboom, "Characteristics of the Euro, the Demand for Reserves, and Policy Coordination Under EMU," in Paul R. Masson, Thomas H. Krueger, and Bart G. Turtelboom, eds., *EMU and the International Monetary System*, Washington, D.C., International Monetary Fund, 1997, pp. 194–224.

Mauro, Paolo, "Current Account Surpluses and the Interest Rate Island in Switzerland," International Monetary Fund Working Paper No. 95/24, Washington, D.C., International Monetary Fund, February 1996.

Maystadt, Philippe, "Implications of EMU for the IMF," in Paul R. Masson, Thomas H. Krueger, and Bart G. Turtelboom, eds., *EMU and the International Monetary System*, Washington, D.C., International Monetary Fund, 1997, pp. 146–153.

Monticelli, Carlo, and Luca Papi, *European Integration, Monetary Co-ordination, and the Demand for Money*, Oxford and New York, Oxford University Press, 1996.

Mundell, Robert, "EMU and the International Monetary System," in Guillermo de la Dehesa, Alberto Giovannini, Manual Guitián, and Richard Portes, *The Monetary Future of Europe*, London, Centre for Economic Policy Research, 1993.

Murray, Stewart, Philip Klapwijk, Hester le Roux, and Paul Walker, *Gold 1997*, London, Gold Field Mineral Services Limited, 1997.

O'Neill, James, Andrew Bevan, and Martin Brookes, "Some Thoughts on the Euro," in Goldman Sachs, *The Weekly Analyst*, No. 96/20, London, May 28, 1996.

Oppers, S. Erik, "Trends in the International Use of the U.S. Dollar," Washington, D.C., International Monetary Fund, June 1995, processed.

Owens, Adrian, "Dollar's Role Under Threat," Julius Baer Investments Limited, London, July 2, 1996.

Padoa-Schioppa, Tommaso, "Policy Cooperation and the EMS Experience," in Willem H. Buiter and Richard C. Marston, eds., *International Economic Policy Coordination*, Cambridge and New York, Cambridge University Press, 1985, pp. 331–355.

Padoa-Schioppa, Tommaso, and Fabrizio Saccomanni, "What Role of the SDR in a Market-Led International Monetary System?" in Michael Mussa, James M. Boughton, and Peter Isard, eds., *The Future of the SDR in Light of Changes in the International Financial System*, Washington, D.C., International Monetary Fund, 1996, pp. 378–386.

Parsons, Nick, "The Euro and Central Bank Reserves," Paribas Capital Markets International Research, *EMU Countdown*, September 9, 1996, pp. 14–18.

Persaud, Avinash D., "The EMU Calculator," JP Morgan, *Foreign Exchange Research*, October 16, 1996.

Persaud, Avinash D., and Dimitris Dambassinas, "Euro, FX Reserves and Vehicle Currencies," JP Morgan, *Foreign Exchange Research*, August 29, 1996; revised September 13, 1996.

Porter, Richard D., and Ruth A. Judson, "The Location of U.S. Currency: How Much of It Is Abroad," *Federal Reserve Bulletin*, 82 (October 1996), pp. 883–903.

Radzyner, Olga, and Sandra Riesinger, "Exchange Rate Policy in Transition: Developments and Challenges in Central and Eastern Europe," in Oesterreichische Nationalbank, *Focus on Tradition*, Vienna, 1996, pp. 20–38.

Rogoff, Kenneth, "Foreign and Underground Demand for Euro Notes: Blessing or Curse?" paper presented to the 26th Panel Meeting of Economic Policy, Bonn, October 17–18, 1997; forthcoming in *Economic Policy*.

Ruskin, Alan, "Euro ≠ D–Mark. Q.E.D. Coming Changes in the Central Bank Reserve Equation," I.D.E.A. Occasional Paper No. 7, London, I.D.E.A., June 1996.

Saccomanni, Fabrizio, "Towards ERM 2: Managing the Relationship between the Euro and the Other Currencies of the European Union," *Banca Nazionale del Lavoro Quarterly Review*, 49 (December 1996), pp. 385–403.

Seth, Rama, and Robert N. McCauley, "Financial Consequences of New Asian Surpluses," *Federal Reserve Bank of New York Quarterly Review*, 12 (Summer 1987), pp. 32–44.

Singapore Foreign Exchange Market Committee, *Annual Report 1996*, Singapore, Singapore Foreign Exchange Market Committee, 1997.

Sjaastad, Larry A., and Fabio Scacciavillani, "The Price of Gold and the Exchange Rate," *Journal of International Money and Finance*, 15 (December 1996), pp. 879–897.

Spaventa, Luigi, "Coexisting with the Euro: Prospects and Risks after Verona," in Peter B. Kenen, ed., *Making EMU Happen: Problems and Proposals: A Symposium*, Essays in International Finance No. 199, Princeton, N.J., Princeton University, International Finance Section, August 1996, pp. 50–63.

Stüdemann, Frederick, "Political Pressure 'Likely to Hit ECB,'" *Financial Times*, September 12, 1997, p. 2.

Svensson, Lars E. O., "The Simplest Test of Target Zone Credibility," *International Monetary Fund Staff Papers*, 38 (September 1991b), pp. 655–665.

Taguchi, Hiroo, "On the Internationalization of the Yen," in Takatoshi Ito and Anne O. Krueger, eds., *Macroeconomic Linkage: Savings, Exchange Rates, and Capital Flows*, Chicago, University of Chicago Press, 1994, pp. 335–355.

Tavlas, George S., *On the International Use of Currencies: The Case of the Deutsche Mark*, Essays in International Finance No. 181, Princeton, N.J., Princeton University, International Finance Section, March 1991.

Tavlas, George S., and Yazuru Ozeki, *The Internationalization of Currencies: An Appraisal of the Japanese Yen*, Occasional Paper No. 90, Washington, D.C., International Monetary Fund, January 1992.

Thornhill, John, "Estonia Likely to Link Its Currency to Euro," *Financial Times*, May 12, 1997, p. 3.

Thorpe, Jacqueline, et al., "Could Euro Bonds Rival the U.S. Market?" in Ruth Pitchford and Adam Cox, eds., *EMU Explained: Markets and Monetary Union*, London, Reuters, 1997, pp. 176–198.

Thygesen, Niels, et al., "The Implications for the International Monetary System of EMU with the ECU as its Single Currency," in ECU Institute, ed., *International Currency Competition and the Future Role of the Single European Currency*, London and Boston, Kluwer Law International, 1995, pp. 117–136.

Triffin, Robert, *Gold and the Dollar Crisis*, New Haven, Yale University Press, 1960.

———, "The Role of a Developing European Monetary Union in a Reformed World Monetary System," in Alexander K. Swoboda, ed., *Europe and the Evolution of the International Monetary System*, Geneva, A. W. Sijthoff for Institut Universitaire de Hautes Études Internationales, 1973, pp. 69–80.

Ueda, Kazuo, "Comment on 'On the Internationalization of the Japanese Yen,'" in Takatoshi Ito and Anne O. Krueger, eds., *Macroeconomic Linkage: Savings, Exchange Rates, and Capital Flows*, Chicago, University of Chicago Press, 1994, pp. 355–356.

U.S. Treasury, *Treasury Bulletin*, Washington, D.C., Department of the Treasury, March 1997.

Wiesman, Gerrit, "More German Banks Are Opening Swiss Units," *Wall Street Journal/Europe*, February 21–22, 1997, p. 14.

Williamson, John, "The Case for a Common Basket Peg for East Asian Countries," paper presented to Conference on Exchange Rate Policies in Emerging Countries, sponsored by Centre d'Études Prospectives et d'Informations Internationales (CEPII)/Association for the Monetary Union of Europe (AMUE)/Korean Institute of Finance (KFI) in Seoul, November 14–16, 1996.

Yam, Joseph, "Hong Kong's Monetary Scene: Myths and Realities," speech before Bank of England Seminar on Hong Kong's Monetary Arrangements through 1997, London, September 10, 1996; published by Hong Kong Monetary Authority, Hong Kong, 1997, pp. 11–20.

Zettelmeyer, Jeromin, "EMU and Long Interest Rates in Germany," in Paul J. Welfens, ed., European Monetary Union: *Transition, International Impact and Policy Options*, Berlin, Springer, 1997, pp. 13–58.

83

PUBLICATIONS OF THE
INTERNATIONAL FINANCE SECTION

Notice to Contributors

The International Finance Section publishes papers in four series: ESSAYS IN INTERNATIONAL FINANCE, PRINCETON STUDIES IN INTERNATIONAL FINANCE, and SPECIAL PAPERS IN INTERNATIONAL ECONOMICS contain new work not published elsewhere. REPRINTS IN INTERNATIONAL FINANCE reproduce journal articles previously published by Princeton faculty members associated with the Section. The Section welcomes the submission of manuscripts for publication under the following guidelines:

ESSAYS are meant to disseminate new views about international financial matters and should be accessible to well-informed nonspecialists as well as to professional economists. Technical terms, tables, and charts should be used sparingly; mathematics should be avoided.

STUDIES are devoted to new research on international finance, with preference given to empirical work. They should be comparable in originality and technical proficiency to papers published in leading economic journals. They should be of medium length, longer than a journal article but shorter than a book.

SPECIAL PAPERS are surveys of research on particular topics and should be suitable for use in undergraduate courses. They may be concerned with international trade as well as international finance. They should also be of medium length.

Manuscripts should be submitted in triplicate, typed single sided and double spaced throughout on 8½ by 11 white bond paper. Publication can be expedited if manuscripts are computer keyboarded in WordPerfect 5.1 or a compatible program. Additional instructions and a style guide are available from the Section.

How to Obtain Publications

The Section's publications are distributed free of charge to college, university, and public libraries and to nongovernmental, nonprofit research institutions. Eligible institutions may ask to be placed on the Section's permanent mailing list.

Individuals and institutions not qualifying for free distribution may receive all publications for the calendar year for a subscription fee of $40.00. Late subscribers will receive all back issues for the year during which they subscribe. Subscribers should notify the Section promptly of any change in address, giving the old address as well as the new.

Publications may be ordered individually, with payment made in advance. ESSAYS and REPRINTS cost $8.00 each; STUDIES and SPECIAL PAPERS cost $11.00. An additional $1.50 should be sent for postage and handling within the United States, Canada, and Mexico; $1.75 should be added for surface delivery outside the region.

All payments must be made in U.S. dollars. Subscription fees and charges for single issues will be waived for organizations and individuals in countries where foreign-exchange regulations prohibit dollar payments.

Please address all correspondence, submissions, and orders to:

International Finance Section
Department of Economics, Fisher Hall
Princeton University
Princeton, New Jersey 08544-1021

List of Recent Publications

A complete list of publications may be obtained from the International Finance Section.

ESSAYS IN INTERNATIONAL FINANCE

170. Shafiqul Islam, *The Dollar and the Policy-Performance-Confidence Mix*. (July 1988)
171. James M. Boughton, *The Monetary Approach to Exchange Rates: What Now Remains?* (October 1988)
172. Jack M. Guttentag and Richard M. Herring, *Accounting for Losses On Sovereign Debt: Implications for New Lending*. (May 1989)
173. Benjamin J. Cohen, *Developing-Country Debt: A Middle Way*. (May 1989)
174. Jeffrey D. Sachs, *New Approaches to the Latin American Debt Crisis*. (July 1989)
175. C. David Finch, *The IMF: The Record and the Prospect*. (September 1989)
176. Graham Bird, *Loan-Loss Provisions and Third-World Debt*. (November 1989)
177. Ronald Findlay, *The "Triangular Trade" and the Atlantic Economy of the Eighteenth Century: A Simple General-Equilibrium Model*. (March 1990)
178. Alberto Giovannini, *The Transition to European Monetary Union*. (November 1990)
179. Michael L. Mussa, *Exchange Rates in Theory and in Reality*. (December 1990)
180. Warren L. Coats, Jr., Reinhard W. Furstenberg, and Peter Isard, *The SDR System and the Issue of Resource Transfers*. (December 1990)
181. George S. Tavlas, *On the International Use of Currencies: The Case of the Deutsche Mark*. (March 1991)
182. Tommaso Padoa-Schioppa, ed., with Michael Emerson, Kumiharu Shigehara, and Richard Portes, *Europe After 1992: Three Essays*. (May 1991)
183. Michael Bruno, *High Inflation and the Nominal Anchors of an Open Economy*. (June 1991)
184. Jacques J. Polak, *The Changing Nature of IMF Conditionality*. (September 1991)
185. Ethan B. Kapstein, *Supervising International Banks: Origins and Implications of the Basle Accord*. (December 1991)
186. Alessandro Giustiniani, Francesco Papadia, and Daniela Porciani, *Growth and Catch-Up in Central and Eastern Europe: Macroeconomic Effects on Western Countries*. (April 1992)
187. Michele Fratianni, Jürgen von Hagen, and Christopher Waller, *The Maastricht Way to EMU*. (June 1992)
188. Pierre-Richard Agénor, *Parallel Currency Markets in Developing Countries: Theory, Evidence, and Policy Implications*. (November 1992)
189. Beatriz Armendariz de Aghion and John Williamson, *The G-7's Joint-and-Several Blunder*. (April 1993)
190. Paul Krugman, *What Do We Need to Know About the International Monetary System?* (July 1993)
191. Peter M. Garber and Michael G. Spencer, *The Dissolution of the Austro-Hungarian Empire: Lessons for Currency Reform*. (February 1994)

192. Raymond F. Mikesell, *The Bretton Woods Debates: A Memoir.* (March 1994)

193. Graham Bird, *Economic Assistance to Low-Income Countries: Should the Link be Resurrected?* (July 1994)

194. Lorenzo Bini-Smaghi, Tommaso Padoa-Schioppa, and Francesco Papadia, *The Transition to EMU in the Maastricht Treaty.* (November 1994)

195. Ariel Buira, *Reflections on the International Monetary System.* (January 1995)

196. Shinji Takagi, *From Recipient to Donor: Japan's Official Aid Flows, 1945 to 1990 and Beyond.* (March 1995)

197. Patrick Conway, *Currency Proliferation: The Monetary Legacy of the Soviet Union.* (June 1995)

198. Barry Eichengreen, *A More Perfect Union? The Logic of Economic Integration.* (June 1996)

199. Peter B. Kenen, ed., with John Arrowsmith, Paul De Grauwe, Charles A. E. Goodhart, Daniel Gros, Luigi Spaventa, and Niels Thygesen, *Making EMU Happen—Problems and Proposals: A Symposium.* (August 1996)

200. Peter B. Kenen, ed., with Lawrence H. Summers, William R. Cline, Barry Eichengreen, Richard Portes, Arminio Fraga, and Morris Goldstein, *From Halifax to Lyons: What Has Been Done about Crisis Management?* (October 1996)

201. Louis W. Pauly, *The League of Nations and the Foreshadowing of the International Monetary Fund.* (December 1996)

202. Harold James, *Monetary and Fiscal Unification in Nineteenth-Century Germany: What Can Kohl Learn from Bismarck?* (March 1997)

203. Andrew Crockett, *The Theory and Practice of Financial Stability.* (April 1997)

204. Benjamin J. Cohen, *The Financial Support Fund of the OECD: A Failed Initiative.* (June 1997)

205. Robert N. McCauley, *The Euro and the Dollar.* (November 1997)

PRINCETON STUDIES IN INTERNATIONAL FINANCE

61. Stephen A. Schuker, *American "Reparations" to Germany, 1919-33: Implications for the Third-World Debt Crisis.* (July 1988)

62. Steven B. Kamin, *Devaluation, External Balance, and Macroeconomic Performance: A Look at the Numbers.* (August 1988)

63. Jacob A. Frenkel and Assaf Razin, *Spending, Taxes, and Deficits: International-Intertemporal Approach.* (December 1988)

64. Jeffrey A. Frankel, *Obstacles to International Macroeconomic Policy Coordination.* (December 1988)

65. Peter Hooper and Catherine L. Mann, *The Emergence and Persistence of the U.S. External Imbalance, 1980-87.* (October 1989)

66. Helmut Reisen, *Public Debt, External Competitiveness, and Fiscal Discipline in Developing Countries.* (November 1989)

67. Victor Argy, Warwick McKibbin, and Eric Siegloff, *Exchange-Rate Regimes for a Small Economy in a Multi-Country World.* (December 1989)

68. Mark Gersovitz and Christina H. Paxson, *The Economies of Africa and the Prices of Their Exports.* (October 1990)

69. Felipe Larraín and Andrés Velasco, *Can Swaps Solve the Debt Crisis? Lessons*

from the Chilean Experience. (November 1990)

70. Kaushik Basu, *The International Debt Problem, Credit Rationing and Loan Pushing: Theory and Experience.* (October 1991)
71. Daniel Gros and Alfred Steinherr, *Economic Reform in the Soviet Union: Pas de Deux between Disintegration and Macroeconomic Destabilization.* (November 1991)
72. George M. von Furstenberg and Joseph P. Daniels, *Economic Summit Declarations, 1975-1989: Examining the Written Record of International Cooperation.* (February 1992)
73. Ishac Diwan and Dani Rodrik, *External Debt, Adjustment, and Burden Sharing: A Unified Framework.* (November 1992)
74. Barry Eichengreen, *Should the Maastricht Treaty Be Saved?* (December 1992)
75. Adam Klug, *The German Buybacks, 1932-1939: A Cure for Overhang?* (November 1993)
76. Tamim Bayoumi and Barry Eichengreen, *One Money or Many? Analyzing the Prospects for Monetary Unification in Various Parts of the World.* (September 1994)
77. Edward E. Leamer, *The Heckscher-Ohlin Model in Theory and Practice.* (February 1995)
78. Thorvaldur Gylfason, *The Macroeconomics of European Agriculture.* (May 1995)
79. Angus S. Deaton and Ronald I. Miller, *International Commodity Prices, Macroeconomic Performance, and Politics in Sub-Saharan Africa.* (December 1995)
80. Chander Kant, *Foreign Direct Investment and Capital Flight.* (April 1996)
81. Gian Maria Milesi-Ferretti and Assaf Razin, *Current-Account Sustainability.* (October 1996)
82. Pierre-Richard Agénor, *Capital-Market Imperfections and the Macroeconomic Dynamics of Small Indebted Economies.* (June 1997)
83. Michael Bowe and James W. Dean, *Has the Market Solved the Sovereign-Debt Crisis?* (August 1997)

SPECIAL PAPERS IN INTERNATIONAL ECONOMICS

16. Elhanan Helpman, *Monopolistic Competition in Trade Theory.* (June 1990)
17. Richard Pomfret, *International Trade Policy with Imperfect Competition.* (August 1992)
18. Hali J. Edison, *The Effectiveness of Central-Bank Intervention: A Survey of the Literature After 1982.* (July 1993)
19. Sylvester W.C. Eijffinger and Jakob De Haan, *The Political Economy of Central-Bank Independence.* (May 1996)

REPRINTS IN INTERNATIONAL FINANCE

28. Peter B. Kenen, *Ways to Reform Exchange-Rate Arrangements*; reprinted from *Bretton Woods: Looking to the Future,* 1994. (November 1994)
29. Peter B. Kenen, *Sorting Out Some EMU Issues*; reprinted from Jean Monnet Chair Paper 38, Robert Schuman Centre, European University Institute, 1996. (December 1996)